VIOLENT FOR PEACE

By the same author

The Rule of Taizé
The Today of God, *Franciscan Herald Press*
L'unité, espérance de vie
The Power of the Provisional, *Hodder and Stoughton, 1968*
Unanimité dans la pluralisme
Taizé, twenty-five years of Community Life; *two records, 30 cm. Jericho*
Taizé, twenty-five years of ecumenism; *one record, 30 cm. Jericho*

VIOLENT FOR PEACE

ROGER SCHUTZ
PRIOR OF TAIZÉ

translated by C. J. Moore

Darton, Longman & Todd
London

First published in Great Britain in 1970
by Darton, Longman & Todd Limited
85 Gloucester Road, London SW7
© 1970 Darton, Longman & Todd Ltd
French edition published by
Les Presses de Taizé, 1968
Printed in Great Britain by
Cox & Wyman Ltd,
London, Fakenham and Reading
ISBN 0 232 51093 8

CONTENTS

Introduction

A THIRD ALTERNATIVE

ALL MEN, whether Christian or non-Christian, are basically aggressive. It is how we use our aggression that matters. Among Christians, it is used in two completely opposite ways.

Some repress aggression and direct it towards an intense spiritual experience. This produces a passive kind of pietism, a lack of involvement with people suffering under oppression. For them prayer is the answer to everything. Anything else would endanger their purity.

At the other extreme, there are Christians who advocate violent, even armed, aggression if it will achieve what they want. They can see no other way of showing their commitment to work against the oppression and exploitation of the poor especially when the oppressor uses an underhand kind of violence.

But the Gospels are not meat for the faint-hearted.[1] Their message is for the spirited. Only those who are aggressive in spirit can possess the kingdom of Christ.[2] Surely, then, there is a third alternative, somewhere between passivity and destructive violence?

Each man has to discover this alternative for himself. Being aggressive for Christ can take many forms, depending on a man's age and situation in life. There is no set path to follow.

Nowadays one often hears so many young people attacking the institutions of the Church. But without some of these institutions, the continuing presence of Christ among men would be seriously weakened.

But don't despair! Many of the young love Christ in a way perhaps never seen before. Prophecy is still vitally important. Between structural deadness on the one hand and sheer nothingness on the other, there is another alternative.

This page is from a diary. This book is made up of a text interspersed with passages from that diary. The passages are not dated and are not in any chronological order. They have been chosen to illustrate the themes touched on in this book. The book itself was written before the disturbances which erupted in France and elsewhere in May 1968. The passages from the diary were written at the time of these events and inserted afterwards.

I

IT'S OUT OF DATE!

Difficulties

IN THE LAST FEW YEARS faith has been severely shaken. It's no use trying to ignore this.

Seething with a destructive kind of violence, some people, when discussing anything to do with the Church, say, 'It's out of date!' They are convinced that the churches, in spite of all their reforms, fundamentally never change and remain a conservative force.

Even the Christian who isn't totally convinced of this has to face up to the confusion which exists everywhere amongst men and women.

To retreat into oneself would be cowardly.

To attack those who reject the disciplines of faith, often for conflicting reasons, would only add to the confusion.

Sometimes our sympathy can express itself only by listening. Because to express an inner conviction just means provoking an argument.

Listen, then, we say to ourselves, and keep on listening; don't let's be provoked! – not because we lack conviction, but because we don't want to impose on others.

DIARY

In the cloister of our church
before community prayers, I often talk
with people who come to the service. This
evening, I was listening to some young
people expressing their violent opposition
to any kind of institutionalism. They
were demanding action, and were very
severe on the Church which, they said,
was dead and beyond repair. If they
cannot recognise some trace of God in
Christians, young people like these cease
to believe in the Church.

At the turn of the century, when the
results of scientific discoveries were
beginning to effect the Christian life,
the relationship between faith and science
had already been discussed. Later on,
however, Christian existentialism
appeared as a possible answer, and it was
in this that the young generation,
twenty-five years ago, placed its hope.

But today this answer is no longer
adequate. The technological age, which is
only just beginning, has challenged
young people to adopt a new approach.

Nowadays we are approaching a neo-
modernistic outlook. More than that, with
the kind of philosophies prevalent at the
moment, we are moving towards a kind of
neo-positivism.

Many people, in order to compromise,
have made the dictates of faith entirely

relative. As far as they are concerned,
everything can be re-examined provided
that man can rediscover his identity in it.
For them, too, communion with God is an
abstraction which they would like to
dispense with in order to identify more
closely – at any price – with mankind.

Suddenly brought up against the conflict
within these young people, I felt deeply
sad all during the liturgy, in the peace
of community prayer. I surprised myself
meditating on death – I, who can spend all
day marvelling at the gift of life!

The numbers of those we call 'ex-Christians' increase more
and more every day, above all young people who, over the
last few years, have turned away from all forms of church
institution. And this means that the Christian, surrounded by
men with a secular outlook, faces a real problem of isolation.

I have the chance, here on our hill-top at Taizé, to hold
discussions with ex-Christians of all denominations and I try
to understand the great change which their questions mean for
men of my age.

But what of the young people who stay in the Church? We
cannot coldly judge them nor can we blame their actions,
even if we find them disturbing.

But we older men, perhaps with much experience behind
us, have to ask ourselves: Have we a monopoly of truth?
Even though these young people use violence to express
themselves and even though we may not recognise ourselves
in them, does this mean that they are completely excluded
from life in Christ? The conservatism and caution of older
people is intolerable when the very future of the Church
depends on taking risks.

Because they are involved in trying to understand and apply Christian commitment in rapidly changing societies, it is hardly surprising that the impatience of young people produces situations of crisis. But the older generation has its weaknesses too. And these become obvious when older people become a burden. However, there have been old men and women full of God's light. We can claim to know something of this ourselves, as contemporaries of John XXIII.

At Taizé, by listening and observing, we sense a great many conflicting aims in the thousands of young men and women who pass through our doors. And no one aim can be singled out; what characterises them is precisely their enormous variety. Youth has the power and the flexibility to contain within itself many possibilities. However, one can perhaps define two general tendencies – indifference and aggression.

Those who are indifferent respond only to immediate interests, all of which are self-centred. They are not concerned with improving human conditions. When they leave the office or the factory at night, nothing interests them except for sports events which are given full coverage by the newspapers and television. Others, well provided for, do no more than pursue the leisure activities available to children of well-to-do families. Communal interests, the good of the city and political matters, they react to with utter indifference, unless they turn these into another kind of game.

The aggressive form the other movement. They want to grapple with life and understand it. Some of them undertake their search with an integrity at times far removed from what older people understand by that word. Others, Christians as well as non-Christians, take immediate action. A few go so far as to dedicate their lives and are drawn spontaneously towards the poorest in society. As for the young generation in countries south of the equator, they have some kind of image of our affluent societies, but they don't share in our wealth. As a result, they feel the kind of bitterness which fosters rebellion.

Aggression or rebellion are often signs of a deep desire to communicate with as many men as possible. In the case of many young Christians, their aim undoubtedly is to find a way of communicating with secular man. They wish to live the life of Christ *with* and *for* all men. They want all men to share in the healing power of God's friendship.

We older people, don't we approve of these activities? Why, then, increase the distance between us by arguing? By censuring young Christians who are occupied in their own search, we are attacking their religious freedom. Time and time again, at the heart of Christianity there appear signs of intransigence and a purist outlook which is hardly indistinguishable from intolerance.

DIARY

It is late at night. I am thinking over some of the things I heard said today by young people. I can see in my mind some of their faces - the clear, though troubled, eyes of a very young girl. I can still hear the rough, but serious voice of a boy who was criticising the Church.

Undeniably their rebellious spirit springs from a real suffering because of the ineffectiveness of this or that church institution. But I am deeply anxious about the disruptions which may result from their aggression.

Yet, over the last two thousand years, people have often spoken about the end of

Christianity. In the year 1000, at the
time of the Renaissance and in the age of
the Enlightenment, there were many people
convinced that it was imminent.

People solve their restlessness through conviction. The
shaking of their faith has matured many young men and
women who, till then, believed out of conformity and were
merely conditioned by their Christian up-bringing. So this
doubt and darkness is not a death for all of them – for some, it
is the beginning of life.

Amongst God's people, certain key issues keep recurring,
and if these are not obscured or distorted, they can become
part of the general direction which history is taking. But when
secondary elements become confused with these issues, progress is delayed and church institutions become static. The
aggression of young people is directed above all at such
lifeless forms of institution, and at everything which fails to
produce concrete achievements. If their insistence sometimes
turns to fanaticism, then we should bear in mind one fact –
that we are in the difficult period of growth.

Are we aware that, far from rejecting commitment to
Christ, the younger generation understand and desire it?
It is true that not so long ago, young people were susceptible
to the arguments of free-thinkers whose object was to remove
Christ from human thoughts. But now a great number of
young Christians will no longer accept façades. They want
to avoid the kind of positions which only exaggerate
the differences between them. They want to abolish all that
is not authentic, to remove everything that constitutes an
obstacle to life itself and everything that hinders real communication.

Any pessimistic summing up of contemporary historical
events is bound to be incomplete. Research gives a man a

certain amount of authority; if he draws conclusions without letting the young answer for themselves, then of course he is bound to reveal his own lack of hope.

DIARY

In Paris, the students are demonstrating. A letter has reached me which includes these lines:

'Will you please pray for us? We feel terribly alone and abandoned. We have made ourselves "stick together" out of loyalty, and now we have woken up to the fact that we are attacked on all sides, from within as much as from the outside. We don't really understand anything any more. We are still too dazed by what has happened to analyse it properly.

'I think it's pointless to talk about it. As for praying, there are times when that's no longer possible.'

While demonstrations are taking place in the universities, students come to Taizé to share their feelings with us. Many different attitudes can be seen in them. The large majority think with a seriousness characteristic of the new generation. A lot of them have lost weight physically. An inner passion burns in them.

Apart from their urge to unite together and to become involved in the life of their universities, a real concern for the future governs their thinking.

I have had three talks with a student from the Sorbonne who took part in all the incidents which happened in Paris during May. At first, he just went to watch, without participating.

I have known him since he was a little boy. In the space of a month, he has grown up in a way you wouldn't have thought possible.

His intellectual honesty is exceptional. One of the first things he said to me when he arrived at Taizé was: 'Over the last month, I have had no way of knowing when I was pretending and when I was being sincere. I tried to find out. After we were beaten up, and especially when we saw others being treated roughly, including girls, our sense of unity just grew by itself; we didn't even think of it.'

From the second talk I had with him, I can remember these words: 'The most difficult thing is to understand what makes up another person, to understand oneself as being amongst other human beings, to reach beyond one's own area of thought.'

How is it that he can remain so calm after all he has been through? Young people of that mettle are demanding. Up to now, we have put young people too much to one side. Either we should build a new society, all of us together, or else there will be a complete break, with two societies running parallel to each other, and we older people will just wait for death completely cut off, in the boredom and plenty of our consumer societies.

For more than a month, now, a majority of students have been intelligently searching for a new relationship between themselves and society. Already they have learnt how to use their enthusiasm to create solidarity amongst themselves, so that they can advance with strength and not fly off like Rimbaud's ship, drunk with novelty.

Whenever attempts are made in society or in a group to repress human dignity and spontaneity, then that society or group is faced with the dangers of rebellion and all its consequences.

The university world, internationally, is being shaken – or is on the point of being shaken – by a ground-tremor which began some time ago in the Latin American universities. The rising importance of the younger generation in society was enough to warn us in advance of the difficulties which we are now experiencing and which will, in fact, help us to develop that much more.

Students have established a consistent position now: they reject any form of society which alienates them; they refuse, during the course of their studies, to be isolated into a special group and, as a result, they want to participate in decisions which affect the whole of society. They see our society caught up in a tangle of technocracy, financial influence, small party politics, and immobilised by the machinery which produces its wealth.

B

They have the vision of a new society which would over-throw the consumer economy, and this vision is expressed in two different ways:

Those who are filled with despair at the way in which society is now organised and structured think that it is first necessary to destroy the present system by a revolution, and that is the only language they have for making themselves understood and for creating a new society. As for teaching others, this would come later.

Most students, however, would rather see everyone sharing in the material goods displayed openly around us, but which remain out of the reach of all but a few in each country.

The inflexibility shown by the first of these reminds us – irresistibly – of the puritan outlook of some Christian preachers who condemn the refrigerator and the washing-machine which, after all, release women from a life of bondage. Through the ages, hasn't it always been the women who were burdened with the jobs that men didn't want to do?

The second group believe in rapid progress towards material plenty as a result of modern automation and technology. But there is a danger of group self-centredness here, because, if their immediate aim is only to distribute all these benefits with-in the frontiers of their own countries, then it will only be achieved at the cost of others becoming poorer and poorer. One result of this, for example in Sweden, is the growth of nihilism amongst young people living without ideals, and an increasing suicide rate.

If progress towards plenty cannot be reversed, is there no way of life, no basis for relationships, which could produce a new society founded on participation and shared benefits, a society which would aim at more than mere consumerism? If they know the meaning of generosity, young people will share their wealth with the poorer nations.

If they don't, our present problems will only re-emerge in a different place and, before long, the poorer nations south of the equator will explode in violent aggression against the richer countries of the north.

Between a consumer society on the American pattern and a bureaucratic society which exists in so many European countries, there is room for a society based on participation. It will not become established by reforms, but by a radical change of direction.

If they want to guide men into a new age, Christians have a path before them: not to let themselves be dragged along by events, but to be ready and waiting for the moments of decision.

Minimising, Maximising

At the heart of our present crisis, one of the causes of tension which separate Christians is the difference between the diametrically opposed attitudes of minimising and maximising.

Both of these attitudes verge on spiritual pride. We should aim at making the words disappear eventually from our vocabulary.

At the one end, we find the 'pure Christian'. He believes he has discovered an interpretation of the Gospels which speaks directly to people. He condemns as Pharisaical anyone who lives by laws and by the commandments of the Church. The weight of tradition, infused with the spirit of past centuries, is too heavy for him to bear. And yet, is it possible for us to live out the Gospels' teaching in our day and age without reference to the major streams of thought which flow through the Church's history and which secure the continuity of Christ's Word among men?

At the other extreme, facing the 'pure Christian', stands the real inheritor of these traditions, the eldest son. No matter what the cost, he wishes to preserve everything he has inherited, even when it conveys the faith only to a small number of people. In every denomination, we find the same argument, the same underlying fear. The slightest alteration of his inheritance is tantamount to throwing it to the winds. The smallest simplification he thinks of as an impoverishment. Now we all agree that some reforms, because they are undertaken cautiously, can be clumsy; but their primary purpose, surely, is to try to reach out to the greatest possible number of men. Far from impoverishing faith, reforms are intended to give Christian traditions an added strength of meaning.

But why do we allow ourselves to become embroiled in conflicts like this? We only separate ourselves from each other even more. The angry impatience of the rebels only strengthens the reactionaries' conviction that change is undesirable.

The rebels' aggression, their nihilism (for nothing except their own principles is valid for them) and the intransigence of the reactionaries (who veto every suggestion of change regardless) – looking at them side by side, we can see the extent to which both are to blame.

In fact, while the two attitudes we describe so inaccurately as progressive and integralist seem to be contradictory, they can spring from one and the same source. Too often, men will use a nicely worked-out argument to disguise their lack of mental agility; thereby hiding from themselves as well as from others the fact that the argument may have deeper implications. Under the pressure of events, it is possible for a Christian who has been protected all his life by a conservative outlook to turn completely against all he has professed. He goes over to the side of those who doubt everything. Nothing holds him, and nothing can claim his loyalties any more.

Between these two extremes, we find the enormous number of those who, in a spirit of poverty, accept certain changes in their outlook. Broadening their minds means, for them, being prepared to find common ground that will enable them to meet with others.

These Christians are setting a path for others. They know that over the years to come, as Christianity progresses, it will have to clear the ground before its feet: certain basic principles must be upheld always, but emphasis must be removed from things that are only secondary.

A true change in our outlook must surely begin with our recognising that all men are conditioned by their early 'formative' years. We must also show sympathy towards those whose lives are governed by quite different terms of reference from our own. We must be aware of the limitations of human nature. We must be ready to entrust ourselves entirely to one certainty greater than any other, a certainty which stems from belief in the eternal.

As men who are trying to reconcile the present with the future, we are caught in the grip of a difficult and pressing task. We need to be constantly alert in following modern currents of thought; at the same time, we must not let ourselves be swept away by any one of these currents.

DIARY

One of our young brothers remarked to me how much our life at Taizé demands that we pay attention to a wide spectrum of events. How right he was!

Here at every moment, our work situates us at the heart of tension, grave tension. So that we can encourage others to seek unity within Christ, we have to listen closely to the inner longings of all kinds of men, of different nationalities and

backgrounds. This duty of ours saves us, I
hope, from ever taking sides.

This evening, during the meeting which
brings us together every day, I gave a
commentary on the text: 'to go so far
as to give his life for Christ'.[1] And
then I said to my brothers: At our daily
meetings, I never speak about our trials,
about the unfounded accusations made about
our life here, which we never answer so as
to avoid useless polemics. I never speak
about our sources of suffering. Why not?
Why do I only talk about the things which
are a source of encouragement. Because I
am afraid of setting up obstacles which
one or another of you may stumble over.
But in spite of that, there is a phrase
repeatedly in my thoughts; it came to my
mind this very afternoon. It is: for
unless the seed dies ...

Courage takes on its greatest value when we fight without
attacking individual men. If Pascal had left us only the Provincial Letters, he would be condemned as superficial and, no
doubt, forgotten. Let that be a consolation to us, thinking of
all the pamphlets men will go on producing in the future.

If we start by provoking great arguments in our efforts to
state the traditional themes of Christian faith in the language
of today, then our sense of humanity will be giving way to a
cold, cerebral orthodoxy which will only drive people away.

But as for the man who dismisses everything – Christian
terminology, prayer, communal life, celibacy – with the
words 'It's out of date!' can he possibly begin to build afresh?
How, rather, can we discover which elements in our traditions

are no longer relevant, and which are essential, fundamental and able to communicate the immediacy of the Gospel to modern man?

One New Change after Another

While conservative Christians are busy closing their ranks in order to protect traditional privileges and safeguards, others believe that the very novelty of certain ideas has a liberating power. But in fact, don't even these new ideas form part of a system? Isn't there a new conformity of language already growing up, which needs to be knocked off its pedestal?

Nothing is more appalling than a doctrinaire mentality! How easy it is to take refuge in some kind of system! Yet the man who gets imprisoned in a system can always be recognised by the same ineradicable sign: he always wants others to be imprisoned with him. He is convinced he is in the mainstream of life but, in fact, everything that constitutes his outlook is already becoming less and less relevant.

The man who says about everything 'It's all out of date!' runs the risk of being caught out in his own game, and also of succumbing to a kind of childishness. While he might try to convince himself he is aiming at true reform, his real motives are simply to create trouble. Obviously, with every step forward, some things immediately become out of date, but this expression can be used with such violent conviction that it can threaten all progress in life.

'It's out of date!' Here, perhaps, we have a brand new cliché and – who knows? – perhaps this saying has already become so standardised as to be meaningless. Every period in history has had its language of conformity. But we don't have to become trapped, through language like this, in new forms of mental paralysis.

If – as some people predict will happen – the Christian of the future will have to live in continual, total doubt, what an exhausting state of mind he will have to endure! But then, in order for us to make progress, we don't have to go on indefinitely restarting from square one; in practice, this is impossible anyway. Surely it's a question of shaking off all that is not essential for living more perfectly in Christ?

In our bodies and our minds is a heritage close and yet distant from us, the mark of the early education which formed our attitudes. We begin our search in life already equipped with a set of positive and negative values. The inexhaustible treasures patiently accumulated over twenty centuries of faith are a part of that inheritance, a part which has a real significance, a part we refer to constantly in our efforts to make ourselves understood through language and communication. What drastic changes have taken place for such an entire area of existence to have survived with continuity! But without that continuity, life itself would wither away.

DIARY

Heard from our Franciscan brothers details of the welcome given to Paul VI at the General Chapter of their Order.

After reading out a message to them, the Pope addressed them spontaneously, saying: 'The road that you must travel is by no means unknown to the new generation with their unconventional tastes; it is the road of anti-conformity'.[2] For a Pope to call on Catholics to be non-conformist will surely be a great cause for rejoicing in many a Protestant home which has fought hard to defend that very principle.

And yet, as soon as non-conformity

moulds itself into a system, it can
become the worst kind of self-deception.
   A non-conformist attitude needs to be
constantly revised. Man finds it easy to
satisfy himself with openly declaring his
beliefs; by doing so, he can excuse
himself from actually putting them into
practice.

How often we find that one cliché simply replaces another!
One new change after another; under modern conditions, this
happens all the more quickly. Nowadays it takes no time at
all for one change to be hidden under the next. By the year
2000, how will man explain his existence?

Already the widespread notion that modern man has no
faith seems to be contradicted by experience. An atomic
physicist was telling me that amongst all those he had worked
with professionally, he had met only two real atheists. Not more
than a few will actually call themselves Christians, but, in fact,
all men are searching.

It is true that the secular life and the life of prayer are not in
conflict. On the contrary, the two are closely related to one
another. God can be discovered through them both.

The emergence of a secular society helps to give a sense of
the provisional. It can be constructive because it releases
energies which had previously been repressed; for there are
religious customs, forms of prayer and certain kinds of church
institutions which all alienate a person and prevent him from
achieving communion either with God or with mankind.

However, there is a considerable difference between understanding this advantage and unreservedly pursuing the goal of
secularisation. Such a pursuit would be naïvely optimistic.

To begin with, it is a fact that whenever religion is up-
rooted from a society, people turn towards the profane and

sanctify it. People cannot bear to live in a void. Thus, they try to fill the void by reviving in other ways the worship which has been abolished. They create ceremonies, solemn inaugurations, civic decorations, flags. . . .

It is not difficult to create this kind of secularism; but in itself, it is just another kind of system. While trying – unsuccessfully – to smash men's idols, the secular system destroys man's spiritual capacity and desire for communion; also, true freedom becomes harder to attain. At this stage, some people demand a Christianity which is non-religious. For these people, prayer is no more than a monologue. They attack the old idea that God can be discovered in a vertical relationship and claim that he can be found only within men themselves and in the interrelationship of one person with another. They situate God in the depths of man's nature, in human communication, and nowhere else. To discover him, one only has to go deep enough into oneself.

But haven't they just imprisoned God once again in a new kind of language? Do these new terms achieve any more than acting as a substitute for the old ones? Before, God could be perceived only in the heights; today, apparently, he is hidden in the inner complexity of the human personality.

Fortunately God is quite beyond the range of all our categories. Christ descended to the lower regions of the earth[3] to offer those who lived before His coming the chance of knowing Him.[4] At the same time, He descended into each and every man. But He also ascended into heaven. He is to be found in every dimension: height, depth and breadth.[5] As long as we keep ourselves ready and watchful, we shall discover Him wherever we look, wherever we go.

DIARY

Here, for two days, we have witnessed a

conference between atheists and ex-
Christians. Dialogue was impossible. Those
who say they have lost their faith are
emotionally aggressive. To be exact, their
aggression seems to turn back upon themselves. They disrupt every attempt at
dialogue. The atheists have good cause for
surprise: why is there such aggressiveness
in people who have given up a life in God?
In these people what snares one has to be
aware of!

But for our own part, we have found,
over the last few years, that the young
people who come to Taizé quickly shed the
traces of a non-religious social system
after attending our community prayer.
Even when we have had up to sixteen
hundred young people gathered here, they
would all come flocking to our community
prayer, three times a day. At night,
there would be a continuous vigil of prayer
in the crypt of the church and there too,
attendance would be high.

Why do they come to pray with us?
Many of them are very interested to know
that a large number of my brothers are
also called to accept the difficulties of
a working life which they pursue amongst
other working men. And these young
people, in their turn, will have to persevere under intolerable conditions,
surrounded by the indifference of so many
men.

What's the Point of Praying any more?

Living in a wealthy society makes us take refuge from certain aspects of life; more than anything else, it can make us listless and bored. When there is no longer any great need to fight for survival, people become apathetic. All their immediate demands are answered; mediocrity governs their life.

In these conditions, the same question is asked everywhere, even by a great number of Christians: What's the point? What's the point of opening one's mind and soul to God, what's the point of praying, when we are all only too aware of the extent of human suffering, disease and war, and with the memory still fresh in our minds of the terror inflicted on millions of men, women and children as they were herded into the gas-chambers?

DIARY

Whenever I have discussions with lay-people, inevitably I hear a voice raised, which asks drily: 'Can prayer ever be more than a monologue with oneself?' After a few moments' hesitation, I try to give an answer:

In communicating with God, man must begin a dialogue, not with himself, but in himself. What is special about this dialogue is that while he is engaged in it, a man consciously places himself before God. Can he always be convinced of God's presence? At times, the presence of God is not perceptible in any way at all. This is faith in its purest state, completely unaided and surrounded by total darkness.

This dialogue, therefore, is kept up within oneself, although it may be unrewarding. But moments will come when, after a long period of prayer, we discover the gentleness of God's presence, and we realise then that his silence was no cause for alarm.

It is true that some people, when they pray, become sidetracked into discussions with themselves. They still believe they are meditating and are deceived irresistibly into thinking that their monologue is a dialogue.

As regards ourselves at Taizé, one of these days I should like to see written up over the door of our church: 'The form of our communal prayer is only provisional, in view of future church unity.'

But if I wrote up, 'Our prayer is out of date', I might just as well lock the church door and throw away the key. Prayer is something that will never be out of date. It belongs to a level of communication which is beyond our control. The only thing that can become irrelevant is a style of language which bears no relation to the life of men.

Young people *do* pray; nowadays, they pray more than they ever have in past generations. So much so, that this fact must be embarrassing to older people who project their own shortcomings on to the young.

DIARY

I was asked by a religious why so many young people participate so enthusiastically in our community prayer here at

Taizé. I told him that twice, over the last few days, we have had the same surprising experience. A group of young people attended our communal prayer for the first time, and then left Taizé. The following day, they had retraced their steps and arrived back here to spend the few days they had intended for a trip to the coast.

A week later, exactly the same thing occurred with another group, in no way connected with the first. A few hours after leaving us, there they were again on our doorstep; and they stayed for several days.

Why? I asked them. They answered: they were seeking God. The most vital discovery they had made at Taizé was our communal prayer. Why? Because our prayer was kept up day after day by men in whom they could perceive a real commitment.

But in addition to this, surely our communal prayer is a moment when time itself changes character and comes to hold the awesomeness of eternity? Through the prayer of the Church, all men together are momentarily released from the constriction of time. This truth is of immense significance to modern men, who are completely taken up with the demands of a civilisation based on productivity and technology.

Here, do we tend to forget the old by praying so much with the young? Nothing

could be further from the truth. Anyone
who has learnt how to listen to the old
will have discovered many a pearl of
wisdom through doing so.

Again, at certain times of the year,
children come and pray with us here; this
is a further, complementary, sign given
to us that all generations possess the
living Word.

In this, as in other things, the profit
is mutual. For a community like ours to
survive from day to day, it needs the
loyalty of many men, women and children.
They come and join their presence to
ours; it is they who sustain our life
here.

Recently, a father and mother visited us
with five of their children. Being
foreigners, they couldn't understand a
word. The persistence of the children in
attending our prayer seemed to worry the
parents. They felt duty bound to put a
stop to it. The children's reaction was
to tell them: 'You can go and finish the
holiday somewhere else. We're staying
here.' Clearly, something more than the
mere communication of words, something
more deeply essential, had penetrated the
understanding of these children.

Because he is free to act for or against God, man can
choose to treat his fellows without respect. But once he finds
himself inured to injustice, can he possibly succeed in
renewing a relationship with God? Without this relationship,

humanity returns to the law of the jungle, with all that it entails.

Who can seriously ask 'What's the point?' with regard to the life of Christians scattered in small numbers all over the world? Their presence saves humanity from some of the awful consequences of brutality and hatred. Christians re-establish harmony in Christ.

They are bold enough to tell men that a source of rest and also of energy is to be found through perseverance in prayer.

It is through persisting in this task as Christians that the aggressive in spirit will possess the kingdom.[6] Often, it is true, their struggle will show no immediate profit.

DIARY

I had a letter from a young brother who has just arrived in a shanty-town in Recife, in the north-east of Brazil, where no one knows what tomorrow holds in store. In his letter he says: 'From what I can see here, it seems that there is a constant effort made to keep the peace and overcome the violence provoked by injustice. One asks oneself: if God exists, why is there evil in the world? If God is good, why is there suffering? If God is good and all-powerful, why is there humiliation and hatred? There's no answer to these questions. We have to look for an answer in the work of living. We arrive back at the saying: 'God is a man in tears.'

Another young brother, who came back here from an open city community, was

talking to me in an obvious tone of
despair about the rising tide of emotions
in Chicago's black ghetto. What can a few
Christians do, helpless as they are in the
midst of a vast modern society so highly
geared to its feverish pursuit of productivity? There are brothers, too, who
come back from Africa and tell the same
story.

All of us can experience this sense of
ineffectiveness. Recently I met a man who
claimed that he had never won a single
victory in his life. I could see in him
all the signs of self-effacement and
marks of deep suffering. As soon as he
closed the door behind him and left, I sat
down and wrote to him the words which I
couldn't bring myself to say to his face:
'Can men of integrity ever succeed in the
battle of the business world? You are a
man of very great integrity. Your victory
is achieved in the unlimited trust placed
in you by those who understand you. I
shall be near you in my thoughts, and also
my prayers, poor as they are.'

The futility of my life! This is the cry which comes from
the hearts of most men.

All men examine the meaning of their life. How much have
others profited by it? For example, there are the parents, the
father and mother, overcome by the sense of failure which
can be sprung on them at an advanced stage of their life. They
have loved their children and created a family unit which is
infused with a very personal happiness. Then a change takes

c

place: for example, the child who has been spoilt suddenly breaks away, and catastrophe strikes.

Any person who has devoted himself or herself entirely to someone else may feel that he has not done enough. In such people, their intensely felt need for sacrifice dominates them to the point where nothing else matters.

Show me the man who can have real faith in the effectiveness of his life! One might perhaps find a mystic who has such highly developed powers that he can assume the burden of all mankind and can genuinely claim to unite men together.

Who, though, can claim to be totally effective? Even the most active of us, in the midst of our efforts, remain inadequate servants,[7] though at the same time, we are cooperating with God.[8] In the dialectic found in the Gospels there is no contradiction in terms: those who go out to sow with tears of futility will reap with songs of gladness.[9] A day comes when the flowers open, and deep joy is known. Then the petals fall; there follows a time of waiting, till the fruit swells. An entire lifetime is barely long enough for all this to take its course.

The greatest perseverance is perseverance without reward, even if the average man educated to the demands of an affluent society is little aware of this truth: men like this have their eye on success, but scarcely is success achieved than their satisfaction gives way to the pursuit of more successes.

DIARY

A meeting with some monks. I try to explain the solidarity between us. Perhaps they can see a reflection of themselves in our community prayer? We haven't invented anything new; we have

simply <u>adapted</u> the prayer of the
centuries.

I point out to them that, at the other
extreme, there are Protestants who look
askance on all liturgical expression;
they may look approvingly on the life led
by our brothers in the poorest areas of
Latin America, amongst the black population in the United States and in the
African nations, but they show less
understanding for the contemplative life,
from which, nevertheless, everything else
proceeds.

But then, each person takes away from us
here what he finds for himself. Our
communal prayer seems to be like a
mosaic which is beautiful for some, but
shapeless in the eyes of others. What is
silent for one strikes a chord in another.
One man may appreciate the psalms above
all; another, the long silent prayer
which follows the Gospel readings;
another the litanies. Again, there are
some who look forward above all else to
the organ-music which ends the service.

Each person extracts his own ounce of
profit. If we thought that a single one
of our visitors - let alone all of them!
- could find everything here equally significant, we would be dreaming of
perfection.

Whatever our situation in life, none of us have any special
privileges where prayer is concerned. We all have to renew

our dialogue with God day by day, and learn over and over again the art of praying. In all of us, there is a part of ourselves which doesn't want to turn towards Christ.

To expect that we shall find prayer easier and easier is also wrong. Some days we manage to say everything in a few words. At other times, our prayer becomes lengthy; we start to utter clichés which have no real substance in them. All our lives, we have to submit to approaching prayer as though we were learning to pray for the first time. There are so many discoveries to be made, and it is so refreshing to be always on the look-out for new finds!

As he grows older, man acquires a measure of certainty which remains with him constantly, even though it may not extend through the whole breadth of his being. After many years, our insistence on our faith brings us to certainty. 'I believe' takes on a meaning which is unequalled in importance by anything else. Yet never do we reach the privileged state when we could forget the phrase which comes in the same breath: 'Help my disbelief . . .'[10]

DIARY

Reflecting on the Last Day and on our coming face to face with Christ - something we're not afraid of - I jotted down the following thoughts which came to me: What will I be asked in that first meeting which I know so little about, except that it will be the first of an infinite number of meetings?

There are some who say we shouldn't be tempted to create what can only be a very premature picture of these final truths; they are probably right. All the same, I tried to answer my own question, and imagined a conversation taking place. I may well hear myself saying at that meeting with Christ:

... as for the Community, what I chiefly loved about it was something which would occur to few people. Most people loved Taizé for its open doors and for the way it entered into dialogue with so many men. But more than this work of sharing, I looked on our waiting, our contemplation, as its greatest quality.

You knew what it was to suffer. You chose, as well, to accept the evangelic call to chastity. You tried to be representatives among men and for men, symbols of the timeless, symbols inspiring men to discover each day afresh and fill it with new life.

This task of waiting was not an intellectual task. It was open to all, and even to the man who thought himself least talented. This task was your greatest strength.

Yes, the essence of your way of life was your own inner struggle, fought through a constant daily renewal of the spirit.

In Conflict with Authority

Many people feel a growing aggression towards those in authority, whom they blame in ways which only cause deeper antagonism between the two.

Now, even the best of men in authority find their responsibility a heavy burden.

DIARY

On television this evening was a
programme in which a bishop was
confronted by a number of lay-people.
One of them was so unsympathetic that he
created an atmosphere of unpleasantness.
    The obvious bitterness in some of them
and their rejection of authority were not
attractive to watch. The bishop won a
little sympathy by being timid; all the
same, the answers he gave could have
been a little warmer.

All too often, we find that church authority has been used as a means of exercising certain rights over 'subordinates'. This attitude has led to power being abused. When church authority identifies itself with temporal power, it no longer inspires the whole body to be a force which is capable of uniting men. It succeeds in maintaining a human organisation which is structurally sound, perhaps, but no more than that. As soon as the authority which is placed in men for the purpose of guiding the Church becomes equated with the principle of monarchy or with the privileges of any government, even in a democratic sense, there is bound to be misunderstanding and serious disharmony.

Surely there must be another approach to power, somewhere between a monarchical structure and a democratic structure?

A minimum amount of structure doesn't in any way restrict the spirit of friendship, so long as each of us within the structure remains aware of his brotherhood with all men.

If a local church refuses to see itself in the likeness of the Body of Christ, it sets itself up as an independent little fellowship. When, on the other hand, every group understands itself as a part within the image of a whole body, then a real communion is established. If the head is severed, the unity of the body will disintegrate. If the members fall out of accord with the head, the entire body decays, inevitably.

In their attempts to counteract this, some try to strengthen authority by placing all the emphasis on its powers; but this can only do the Church great harm.

Today, obedience and authority are no longer understood in terms of power, but in terms of communion.[11]

DIARY

I was telling some of my brothers about a little incident which has just happened; for the first time ever, I let drop a remark about the Franciscans who are at Taizé.

One of the brothers predicted that, over the next few days, I would work hard to make the Franciscans forget what I said. He certainly knows how my mind works! I believe it important that we should respect the independence of others; on the other hand, this concern of mine can often stop me from taking action.

Authority must create communion. It is also a work of mercy. Without it, there would be no hope of unity in our community. Yet how much longer must we listen to people talking about 'princes' of the Church, or about 'great churchmen'? Such talk is wrong because, amongst God's people, there is no division into great and small. All of us, equally, are men striving to love and to serve.

If authority means communion, it is above all because of its pastoral character. It watches over the spirit of solidarity which must be kept alive in the body as a whole. Of course it is possible for a man to live the Gospel message without being physically united to the whole body, but only at a terrible price! Freedom can rapidly become confused with personal necessity and lead a man to isolate himself and, in the very name of evangelic purity, to work alone, instead of acting as a force within society.

For us to keep the emphasis on communion, those in authority will have to detach themselves as much as possible from the preparatory stages which precede any important decision, by placing the issue first of all in the hands of groups within the Church. In this way, any steps which are taken are not determined only at the highest levels of the Church. It remains for the authorities to make the final decision once it has taken shape at ground-level.

This ministry of sustaining communion, a ministry fulfilled by a man, has remained unchanged through the centuries: it has always meant addressing the living word to all men, the word which speaks in the innermost depths of each man[12] and calls him to turn his eyes towards a new goal. The spirit of rebellion which is in us all, is unwilling to listen to this word. It is far easier for us to reject the authority of the man who is speaking and pretend that we are completely free.

DIARY

Those who wield authority know only too well the real difficulties that can arise when they have to impose a harsh decision, or when they find themselves humiliated.

A man lays himself open to humiliation to the extent that he takes risks, for every act of courage is met with criticism from some quarter.

But too much exposure to humiliation can wear our spirits down, and, when this happens, even the closest of us to Christ will be tempted to look for purely psychological support. Sometimes we find it in our own self-esteem, encouraged by whatever honours are conferred on us; or else we get into the habit of defending our actions automatically. In this way, without realising it, we begin to glorify ourselves.

And what about the man who has laboured at writing a huge work which will go on living even after he dies? What significant impact will he make? At most, he may influence a few people here and there, but not many. In the history of the churches, the greatest of men have attracted only a limited number of admirers; if there are exceptions, they are rare. Why, then, do we find everywhere this urge to shine brilliantly in the eyes of men? If we look closely, we see that the number of disciples who are prepared to keep a weak light burning is very small indeed. Yet this is still a tare which is found growing in every church.

Another source of redress for those in authority is for them to turn against the people who have humiliated them. If entered upon, this is a path which leads straight to misery, because they begin to find hostility wherever they look. Everything becomes blacker and blacker. They forget that it is the peacemaker who is called blessed.[13]

There are times when we all feel like shouting out, 'Stop fighting yourself, trust in God's goodness and in your true friends for all the reassurance you need so desperately.'

Surely, no matter how much humiliation we suffer, every single one of us must take up our cross at the start of each day, hiding from those around us the pain we are bearing?

The Ordeal of Community Life

Amongst other things, the idea of vocation to the communal life is dismissed by some people with the comment, 'It's out of date.' They raise serious questions:

Why are those who live in communities so hesitant about introducing necessary reforms? Why do they resist and refuse to compromise?

Why do they make their life more difficult by segregating the old from the young? They no longer symbolise true brotherhood. They spend their time bewailing the indifference shown to them by the world at large.

What signs are left of those early monks who took vows

which committed them for life to serving everyone who had
need of them?

DIARY

I had a very moving talk with a friend of
mine, a priest, who believes he is doing
a service by helping a certain religious
to leave his Order, which, as far as my
friend is concerned, is a dying
institution. And yet there are two and a
half thousand men who belong to that
Order.

I offered him an explanation of what lay
behind the dramatic upheaval of the
Reformation. There came a moment when it
seemed hopeless to expect any reforms at
all in Catholicism, and there was utter
despair. A fresh start was attempted,
independently. It was God's will that the
Holy Spirit should breathe upon this new
creation of man, for He loved his own far
too much to abandon them. But, at the
same time, the image of Christ's body and
its unity became obscured in the eyes of
men.

A few days ago, another priest was
assuring me that a monastery he had
visited for a time was doomed and had no
possible future. And yet any institution,
however ailing, can still count on its
members, on those who give it life. In
this particular case, as it happens, I am
personally convinced - because I know the

man – that the spiritual father of the monastery mentioned by the priest possesses all the qualities needed to inject new life into his community.

Every change in us comes from within. Our mental habits are conditioned by our inner selves. It is on the innermost levels of our being that we experience our continual conversion to Christ, through constant forgetfulness and denial of Him.

Clearly, we must use every possible means to reform the old, inherited, structure. But in spite of all the splendid façade put on it by reforms and for all its inner beauty of logic, if this structure is not supported by men of generous spirit, then it will fail to be a source of inspiration and light.

One of my brothers, living with an open community in Chicago, wrote to me about the crisis which 'communal life' is undergoing in the United States. He ended his letter with these words: 'Most of the new reforms indicate such a reaction against the past for its own sake that I'm afraid they'll lead to disaster.'

In North and South America above all, communal life is going through an ordeal by fire, from which it cannot emerge unscathed. But why be so pessimistic as to declare that it has lost all its value?

We can already foresee that the bond it has with the Christian laity will give communal life a new start. At this moment in time, lay-people are full of an exceptional energy and dynamism.

There is a sector of the laity which refuses to be shaken by present events. In union with others, this lay-sector believes firmly in the contemplative vocation, and they are a strong-minded group of people, capable of great projects and great daring, which gives many priests and pastors the strength to hold firm in the middle of confusion. Often, it is their sanity which has restored balance and saved priestly vocations which, but for their support, would have foundered in rebellion or in sheer defeatism.

DIARY

Visited parishes in a large town in the south of Italy. Made contact with a university chaplaincy.

On Sunday morning, all the churches were packed with people. The congregation responded happily in Italian; there was a sermon based on a text from the Bible. Some of us - myself included - have certain misgivings about this or that part of the Christian world; I wonder, now, if they are justified? When the Holy Spirit is at work, which can be clearly seen in our present efforts to reform, we should not be surprised when we find large numbers of lay-Christians, in spite of their reputation for formality, making use in an exciting way of all it has discovered.

But, on the other hand, in regions where faith has disappeared, as in our

own area around Mâcon, amongst others, no
one has any real awareness of the sacri-
fices endured by the pastors and small
handfuls of lay-people, tirelessly,
generously, in conditions like those of
the desert. The witness borne by their
life finds no echo in society around them.
What patience will be needed before new
life can grow out of such terrible
aridity!

Unless there is a mutual exchange between committed lay-
Christians and those men and women who are called to be
contemplatives, neither side will be able to develop fully. If
solidarity is confined to the ranks of the laity or, alternatively,
to those of the 'religious', in either case a vital dimension of
church unity will have disappeared.

For the modern laity, caught up in technology and a world
of symbols, communities can be a sign of eternity.

To enrich communal life, however, members of a community should go, a few at a time, to spend periods in the
heart of society, amidst the laity.

By spending alternate periods in small open communities,
at the centre of city life, and also by visiting their family
homes at regular intervals instead of going straight back to the
community, the life of religious will become more balanced
and more human.

DIARY

These last few days, we have had some of
Charles de Foucauld's 'spiritual family'
staying here; it has been an opportunity

both for us and for them to reaffirm our
longstanding friendship.

If church unity had been a reality in
the early days of Taizé, then there would
have been no hesitation; Père de
Foucauld's family would have joined us
here in our task of waiting. But the call
to ecumenism separated us, and our paths
went different ways.

Then, at a certain moment in time, we
felt the need to emerge from our life of
silence and extend a welcome to all men,
and in particular to the young.

In those early days, there was a woman
who spoke her mind to us quite plainly.[14]
She said that for all our brothers to
become dispersed in small houses would be
a denial of the whole meaning which
Christians place on the visible symbol
of the community. In a world where dis-
persion was the rule, she thought that his
symbol was absolutely essential. Perhaps
she was foretelling the kind of conditions
which we see regulating modern life,
which create widespread disunity between
men and societies, and which drive men to
seek the quiet which religious houses can
offer them in times of difficulty.

Some people think that, at Taizé, we are rather more
privileged than most institutions, as if we had a wider margin
of freedom than others elsewhere.

It is quite true that we have refused to create organisations
and institutions centred on ourselves here. Nevertheless, we

have close relationships with others, relationships which do, in fact, restrict our liberty, because they make us hesitate to undertake new schemes without the participation of others.

There are times in our existence when our field of freedom becomes narrowed, and then broadens again. We have to accept that there are roughly defined boundaries within which we are free to work.

When we come up against these boundaries and find that the space left for working is minimal, often this can cause disappointment. But we are given courage to go on, day after day, working in a confined space, by the fact that there *is* space and we *can* create within it.

Artistic creativity has the same character; just as the work of art is fashioned according to certain rules and precise laws, everything that is built within the Church of God is disciplined by its relationship with the whole. This is one of the ways in which we are all called to live through the universal character of the Church.

DIARY

I have been more moved this evening than on any other occasion this year. I was visited by some friends who come from Poland; the conversation was proceeding quietly enough until I heard them say that amongst all the very great difficulties they have to contend with, in their efforts to maintain some kind of balance between Marxism and the Church in their country, they constantly look to a small religious community, modern in spirit, which is a constant source of hope to them.

To hear such a tremendous declaration
made about ourselves fills me with
surprise, not to mention uneasiness.
I cannot subscribe to everything that they
said. No Christian can claim to have
achieved what he set out to do, even when
he hears tell of some success he is
responsible for.

The incident inspired me to address all
my brothers, later, during our meeting,
with the following words:

Who are we? A group of men who had no
say in choosing one another, and who are
striving to reconstruct something of the
character of the earliest Christian
community.

Who are we? A small, vulnerable community, held up by an irrational hope,
the hope of creating harmony between the
children of baptism and between men
everywhere; a community of seventy men,
Christians, called on to do a task which
is quite beyond them, and who, in spite of
their limited numbers, try to answer every
appeal made to them, no matter from
which direction.

Nothing could come of this attempt if
we were not, in the first place, a community of men who have dedicated
themselves, each within himself, to
persevering to the end in a struggle for
Christ and for ourselves which is
frequently gruelling and hard.

At any time, any one of us can become a

D

victim of pride, pride in our own life.
At that moment vanishes what was a simple
response to a call, and in its place
emerges something else, a need for power,
a manner of glorifying ourselves,
together with hostility towards everything
in us or around us which still reminds us
of that first call.

Persevere! This is one of the spiritual
messages we hear repeated daily, in our
age when more and more is being called
into doubt. We cannot be expected to
stand firm if, all the time, everything is
exploding like fireworks about us;
blinded by it all, how could we hope to
keep in touch with reality? But the good
thing about these fireworks is that the
odd one, occasionally, can light up our
hearts with joy, and this helps us to turn
back, tirelessly, to the work of persevering.

We must persevere first of all, with
those nearest to us, which is the first
step towards trying to unite with all
mankind.

Who, then, are we? A tiny community
which is often buffeted, but which is
always able to find its feet again
because it is supported by a presence
which is greater than itself, and which
joins it to eternity.

Who are we? To sum up in a word our
present situation: we are a gathering of
people with many human failings but a

community visited by One who is other than ourselves.

Opposed to Commitment

There are many people who are afraid of committing themselves for life; there are some, even, who oppose the very idea of commitment, who would like each event in life to be experienced free of the discipline of a lifelong loyalty, and each day to be lived independently and purely provisionally.

This attitude strikes above all at the evangelic call to celibacy.

DIARY
—

A pastor was asking me what had been the greatest hardship for us. What has been hardest for us to bear is intolerance, particularly when we come across it in our own Churches.

Why is it that, since earliest times, people have refused to admit that a man has a vocation when he says 'yes' for life to a call he hears? Four centuries after the Reformation, we have decided to break the silence and answer the call to celibacy. But time and time again, we hear the same argument repeated to us: the freedom of the Holy Spirit is too vast for you to reduce it to a decision which commits you for life.

To begin with, we used to renew our commitment to celibacy annually, until we came to see that the Holy Spirit was

strong enough to bind men for life when,
for Christ's sake, they were willing to
persevere in the state to which they were
called.[15]

This was a gift, the final gift, which
we could not see, then, in all its significance. It was only long afterwards
that we discovered it enabled us to open
our doors to all men.

Here I should add a little incident
which was important in my own life.
Shortly before my first communion, I
approached my father, who was a pastor, to
try to make him postpone the date. But he
could not risk the criticism which would
follow if he excused his own son from an
obligation fulfilled by everyone else; at
Easter, every boy and girl who had
reached the age of sixteen would
make their first communion, without
exception.

In the end, I had to submit to his
judgement. I accepted that he was only
doing his duty; I would not worry about
the expense to myself.

The day I made my first communion, my
father read me these words from the
Gospel: 'Be faithful until death, and I
shall crown you with the crown of life.'[16]

It was only much later that I paid full
attention to these words, a part of the
Living Word which, in this case, perhaps,
was not entirely without fruit as it found
its way back to God.[17]

The Catholic clergy have not suffered so great a shock since the time of the Reformation. Many believe that priestly celibacy is at the root of their troubles. Psychiatrists maintain, though, that this is not the only cause: 'Clearly, celibate life involves certain tensions, frustrations and problems, as is rightly pointed out. We must not forget that married life has just as many strains, although of a different kind completely. To state it simply, it would be extremely naïve to believe that a human being can find happiness only in marriage, and that celibates are necessarily unhappy and unbalanced. This is a rigid and somewhat childish notion contradicted by our broadest experience.'[18]

No, the present crisis principally concerns the ministry itself. In the Protestant Churches, where most pastors are married, there is equal unrest. It is expressed in a violent reaction against the image of the ministry as an ecclesiastical function, and against the clericalism which has grown up, in the Protestant Church as well as others, over the centuries.

Both pastors and priests today are searching for the essential character of their ministry; they refuse to act as officials.

Some of them argue that they must earn their living by working at a trade, and they find the perfect balance in their life by undertaking a purely secular job. Through working in society beside other men, it becomes possible for them to live another life apart, as demanded by the consecrated role of the ministry. But others find that the ministry itself provides them with a valid and complete job of work. From now on, we shall surely see more than one interpretation of this role in practice.

DIARY

A number of pastors from Geneva ate at my table. They were telling me about their

catechumens, who receive instruction
during the years they spend at state
schools, and then a further two years of
catechism. At this stage, they make their
first communion. Only three or four per
cent continue to practise their religion
within the Church.

In some of the younger pastors I could
detect a certain amount of concern. They
said to me: 'There is nothing more frus-
trating than to be looked on as church
officials. The pastoral duties we have to
fulfil, like baptisms, marriages,
funerals, can become an intolerable
burden in the end. Why aren't we allowed
to earn a living like other men? If we
were, the time we devoted to the ministry
would be much fuller.'

Can a man who has become a symbol of contradiction by
committing himself to celibacy, decide to relinquish his role,
in which he is the Living Word? Surely he is called on
to regain a spirit of waiting, a sense of encounter, within
himself?

This he can only do through living in Christ for men. If he
forgets this, then chastity becomes burdensome, in a way
which must afflict any man who remains conditioned by
society around him.

If the contemplative life has been slowly stripped of value,
chastity has suffered total shipwreck; the irreversible and
definitive sacrifice it demands leads inevitably to apathy or
revolt in those who have taken it on their shoulders.

DIARY

At my table today was a very old friend, a
Protestant layman; a man of uncommon
frankness. He informed me that one of his
girl pupils is going to marry a religious
who is leaving his order after twelve
years of community life.

The conversation moved on to other
topics, but I felt a terrible inner
sorrow. We could not be expected to react
in the same way, he as a director in
charge of his teaching, myself as the
brother of my brothers.

What I would give to be able to help
men to remember their initial moment of
decision, and find a way of remaining
faithful to their commitment until the
very end of their life!

There have been times in my life here
when, anxious to help all those in
difficulty, I gave most of my time to
visitors from outside, to the point of
neglecting close contact with my brothers.
Yet this was essential, since by meeting
people from outside the community, a
mutual change in outlook takes place.

The same preoccupation is felt in the
open community in Chicago where many of
my brothers live, together with
Franciscans. They had nowhere in their
house for putting up visitors, and so they
hired an extra apartment. Why? Simply for
the purpose of receiving priests and

religious who had abandoned their vocations. By giving them hospitality, the community hopes to inspire them to reconsider what they are doing.

During the Vatican Council, I came to the rough conclusion that the Catholic Church would be able to withstand any reform except one. It would split right down the middle if priests who were already consecrated were allowed to marry. After a thousand years' alliance between the office of the priesthood and celibacy, too many nerves would be exposed by such a change; Catholics aren't ready for it yet.

All the same, there is no doubt that, in Latin America and Africa above all, chastity can be an impossible ideal for some priests living in isolation, in spite of all their pastoral fervour. I am often amazed when I think of these men.

I ask myself, as well, why the Catholic Church is so slow in permitting deacons to be married men. Possibilities such as these have yet to be explored in pastoral life, and, through them, the Church of tomorrow will see an enormous increase in vocations.

For young people, sex is no longer a forbidden activity. Since they use it at pleasure, without any restrictions, it has come to mean less.

To compensate for this, there are other energies apparent in the young, and new forces of aggression. Usually these are channelled into attacking the older generation, because of everything it has failed to give them.

But young people forget the real significance of sex in life. Sexuality extends through the whole personality, underlies it and motivates behaviour in many different ways which are visible both in married life and in celibate life.

In order to be fully human, we must be aware of the nature of our whole being. Our knowledge of our own humanity is supremely important if we wish to offer ourselves daily, as an offering which is forever new.

We must make all our reserves accessible, all our inner forces, emotions and unsounded depths where there springs an unsuspected and rich source of vitality; all this must be placed at Christ's disposal, in full knowledge of what we are offering him.

In the celibate life, a man submits the most personal offering possible; by doing so, he allowed Christ to work in the very depths of his personality. He seeks an encounter with Christ, the encounter with the resurrected Christ, so as to go out and encounter all mankind.

In the service of these demands, the celibate fills every moment of his life with their reality, every day and every night, bearing his isolation and whatever bleakness oppresses him. And so he comes to know the Absolute which is to be found in this encounter.

DIARY

I have never been so well prepared as I was for today, June 29, because today, a number of priests were ordained, among them, friends of mine.

They are entering the ministry at a very young age. They will have to face a society which is not interested in their commitment. They will not have the protective support of the whole body of the Church which, in the past, was an important prop for the clergy.

They will come to know the restless motion of time, bringing disheartedness, weariness, when the brilliance of hope is burnt out and left behind.

Through the long course of their life, only holiness will lead them past every obstacle. Without holiness, all their efforts will turn back upon themselves, or will be spent in surrounding them with small sources of comfort. Holiness alone will unite them directly with Christ, and with all men who bear witness to the faith.

The provincial of a religious order came and spent two days here. He had returned from Nigeria where he had lived near an open community founded by Taizé. He remarked to one of my brothers there, who had passed through higher college and who was working as a bricklayer on a building-site, 'Your work is for the future good of society.'

He was struck by the answer which the brother gave him: 'The people around us here don't know what a Christian is. Our first duty is to live with the holiness of Christ himself. All the rest, our contribution to progress, follows naturally.'

2

THE WAY OUT

New Divisions

THE TWENTIETH CENTURY is called the 'age of ecumenism'. Is it really a time of unity, though, a time of reconciliation?

Recent years have produced divisions on every level, conflicts and new factions, all separating men. There is a division between the northern hemisphere, with its wealth of ideas and its affluent societies, and the southern hemisphere, descending into poverty, with its vast areas of ferment, resolutely opposed to becoming by-products of western civilisation. There is a division amongst theologians. A division between the generations. And there are so many people, too, nowadays, who are led by their own fervour to condemn other attitudes in Christian thought, with the result that the idea of religious freedom is meaningless to them.

There are times when we feel that the phrase 'separated brethren' could apply equally well to the members of one and the same Church.

We can enter easily into dialogue with non-Christians; but in the case of other Christians, we are still not past the stage of religious intolerance. It is through coming closer to non-Christians and sharing with them that we can sometimes get beyond that stage with our fellow Christians.

DIARY

Divisions and splits, of whatever kind, in a community are a sign of sectarianism.

Why is there always some kind of seg-regation at work in the Church of God? Once it was the older generation excluding the younger generation. Now the whole process is going into reverse; and it isn't good to hear young people casting doubt on the faith of 'dear old ladies'.

This reminds me of something said by the grandmother of one of my brothers: 'I am never bored, because He is always there.' As she spoke, she showed us a picture of Christ on that evening in Emmaus.

I am never bored. I used to hear my own mother say the same.

They can still surprise us, these older women who are way ahead of the youngest of us in their courage and in the strength of their commitment.

Why is there no peace amongst the people of God?

Peace disappears amongst Christians when all our instincts developed by conflicts past and present reduce us to examining one another's wrongs. In this state of mind, we are incapable of approaching one another and saying:

I am partly responsible myself for the separation between us. I wanted to make Christ's Church purer, less rigid, less cluttered with the weight of years, of centuries. But I could not succeed, because I tried to achieve this without you; I did not understand you, which is to say that I did not love you. Now everything is clearer to me. I see where I went wrong. The very things I wanted to make purer in my own Christian society have now lost their brilliance for the society of mankind.

If we are not visibly united and one, how can we ask men to believe that it is the one Christ who inwardly inspires us all? We must throw aside our quarrels of the past and all that separates us now, and become, all together, the energy that pushes towards peace.

But how can we cure our own blindness? How can we make ourselves realise that we are all responsible for our separation? Who will show us that for every division, like every divorce, blame can be attached to both sides?

Can we afford to be interested in anything now which is not directly concerned with achieving unity in Christ and with building the City of men?

From the earliest times, Christians have called one another to peace with these words: 'Begin the work of peace in yourself so that, at peace, you may carry peace amongst others.'[1]

Without this principle, which is at the heart of Christian life, everything begins to shake and fall. Even the work of ecumenism can turn into a battleground, amongst traditionalists and reformers alike. We can see the signs of this in many Christians who have found it a hardship to remain in God's Church, and who have not been able to accept, patiently, the trials involved.

DIARY

Some theology students were telling me that they cannot carry on with the existing structures of thought. They asked me: 'What can we create as a way out?'

I looked at their young faces; one of

them, Pierre, I think is as stable a
young person as you could hope to find.
Another of them, I feel, is very deeply
disillusioned.

I tried to answer them by saying that
we cannot weather a crisis except by
remaining within the issues which produced
it. If we try to evade the trials of the
moment by creating an alternative, we lose
our capacity to adapt.

Why is it that our 'age of ecumenism' has not yet shown any visible proof of unity?

Is it because, in the western world, our habits of intolerance are so ingrained after four centuries that we have lost the impulse to extend a welcoming hand, to show goodwill, to show a spirit of forgiveness?

Is it because 'we have just enough religion to make us hate, but not enough to make us love one another'?[2]

Our conscience prompts us to say what we think about Christians whose attitudes differ from ours; but should this prevent us from praying for them all, and even for those who condemn our own attitudes?

When our conscience passes judgement, we are involuntarily obeying a law of human nature, not a law which applies only to Christians: the law by which we all experience guilt. It was an agnostic who wrote that it had taken him a full year of depression before he finally cast off the hard encased guilt of twenty-five years.

Unity between Christians, like unity in marriage or in any kind of community, does not come from making demands on one another. There is nothing more destructive to oneself than being concerned for the other person simply for the sake of changing that person.

DIARY

A friend said to me: 'You are a realist.
Why, then, do we never find you writing
about things you disagree with, or
criticising features either in Protestants
or in Catholics?'
  I replied:
  Don't ever forget that we have behind us
a long history comprised of centuries of
misunderstanding. We have developed a
certain sensitivity, certain mental habits
have been formed in us. Accusations have
flown back and forth between Christians of
different confessions, and none of them
has ever produced a change in outlook, and
none of them has ever brought the conversion which was wanted any nearer.
  As far as the Catholic Church is concerned, the answers are taking shape. But
Catholics, must reach the answers which
are right for themselves.
  As things stand at present, if we were
to apply too much pressure in trying to
close the gap in the ways we thought best,
it would only become wider, not any
narrower.
  For my own part, I hope I shall never
condemn anyone. This does not mean
agreeing with what is wrong, but waiting
for the right moment to state one's mind.
  By learning all that discretion has to
teach us, we can profit fully from the
real forces within us. The human

personality develops most of all through
sharing confidences; only in confidence
can everything be said.

By keeping an open welcome ready and
placing no limits on our goodwill, we
can one day move on from the stage of
dialogue to the stage of sharing. By
achieving this with our fellow
Christians first of all, we will then be
ready to approach the agnostic and the
non-believer.

When a Church enjoys a majority in a country, we can
easily understand how it can become intolerant. But why are
some minority Christian Churches so intolerant? Why do they
show such a lack of respect for other individuals' rights, as
soon as they are confronted with a point of view which does not
conform to their own patterns of thought?

This can be explained, perhaps, by the sociological law that
a minority is always afraid of being absorbed; it reacts
against any movement at all towards unity.

Whether the minority is Catholic or Protestant, the reaction is the same; such Churches are only capable of understanding up to a point the convictions of others. They seize
everything that approaches them and scrutinise it, out of self-
defence.

And so one generation succeeds another; the sons, even in
attacking their own fathers, are infected with the same
intolerance, no less violent than before, and no matter what
radical changes their ideas undergo, the principle of intolerance remains the same.

DIARY
───

A French priest was telling me how much

easier it was for him to come to terms
with the pastors and lay-people of
Churches which had enjoyed a majority in
their country ever since they were
founded. With these, he found it possible
to advance on common ground. But on the
other hand, Protestants who looked upon
themselves as a minority threatened by
Catholicism would tend to keep at a
distance.

Many people are surprised that Taizé, situated as it is in the French religious world, has escaped attack. It is true that we have never had to put up with attacks on our integrity, but this does not mean we have escaped severe criticism for many of our activities.

Some Protestants have alienated themselves from us; but, equally, Catholics were afraid because we are a product of the Reformation.

We are the sons of two families, who have inherited the consequences of a divorce which took place four centuries ago. We would like to reconcile our father-family, the family of our fathers, the Churches of the Reformation, with our mother Church, the Catholic Church. We can never be a party to condemning one of them in order to quieten the fears of the other. We hope that we shall never say anything contrary to the love we hold for both of these families, these Churches.

DIARY
___

A few days ago, after answering the
questions put to me by a group of
people from some thirty countries, I

E

decided to ask them, in turn, what
impressions they had received of us. They
thought for a while, and then said: 'Would
it be fair to say that your community
reflects, on the one hand, a vocation of
suffering, and, parallel to that, the
freshness of life which we can find in
the Gospels? If we are right, we have only
one thing to say: stay as you are!'

The divisions in Christianity today will have consequences
as enormous as those inflicted by the great split in the sixteenth
century, unless we see the emergence of men and women who
are determined to reach out beyond the difficulties.

But they cannot hope to be peacemakers unless they are,
before anything else, men and women living for the encounter
with Christ, the Man amongst men, throughout the length of
their days and the hours of their nights.

When this encounter occurs in us, we are filled with awe.

But we cannot rest there. Before long, we are called by
another demand, the demand to encounter man, even the man
who does not share our faith, even the man who attacks our
faith.

Because in the face of each and every man, 'above all when
tears and suffering have rendered it transparent',[3] we witness
the face of Christ Himself.

The Patience of the Younger Generation

In some parts of the world, the spirit of church unity has
produced enormous steps forward and separated Christians
have really come much closer together. This has an importance which no one can overlook. For many, it is like the
coming of spring after a long winter, and they feel duly

grateful. Like the winds of spring, this ecumenism re-awakens life that was dormant; it makes us face one another and be truthful. Agnostics, too, feel its effects, and are moved by the same sincerity which we search for.

And yet it would be wrong to think that all is bliss. In the minds of the young certain misgivings arise, and they argue: If ecumenism is just another idea, what's the use? If it is only meant for talking, it will create new tension. If it does not lead on from here to produce actions, it is valueless.

Dialogue can reach a point where it echoes in emptiness. There is a time for dialogue, but then comes the time for co-operation, for real encounter.

Those young people who have most appreciation of this are willing to wait and be patient. Their attitude is:

In thinking of ourselves as Christians, we keep thinking in terms of a family united in faith, and all our terms of reference are local and historical. This paralyses us. We want an ecumenism which will help us to live on from today, though without destroying the great links with the past life of the Church.

Once Christians cease to feel the urgency of establishing a visible proof of unity, can ecumenism have any purpose? How can people say that since we have been separated for centuries, unity must be the work of centuries? Are we living the message of the Gospel for our own times if we persist just because of our past history in putting off the union of Christian communions which is so essential as an inspiration towards the union of all men in one brotherhood?

We are all the victims of four centuries of separation. We want there to be a reconciliation, and we want it to happen soon, because if it doesn't, we shall be professing an ecumenism which has no staying power, and which will not interest the next generation in the slightest. The new generations are watching out for anything that means real progress; but anything that disguises compromise, they will turn from and walk quietly away.

This is the sort of enthusiasm we hear from young people who go on to say:

In our love for the Body of Christ, the Church, we are one with her in her failings as well as her strengths. We want to live in a spirit of forgiveness with separated Christians, eradicating the past, living in the present, which is the only way to talk about forgiveness without denying the Gospel in the same breath.

Like John XXIII, we no longer want to be involved in an historical analysis of who was right and who was wrong.[4]

We no longer want to be restricted by narrow loyalties and made to look continually back on ourselves and on our local history.

We want to live in Christ for all men and, through a Church which is once more united, work for a new and loving relationship between all men.

We cannot continue to accept segregation between members of different confessions, which is as hypocritical as racial segregation. If we are not forced out of our separation by following the ideas of ecumenism, and if these ideas do not succeed in turning our hearts of stone into hearts of flesh,[5] what is the use of pursuing them?

We are only too aware of the infection which has spread through Christian societies, and worked on them for four centuries, called 'self-defence', 'self-justification', 'controversy'. This is an endless process by which every new dimension is drawn back into the old structures; and this process could turn ecumenism into no more than just another new church institution, properly controlled by each church authority so that, in each case, it would allow the Church to draw back into itself even more. This habit is also a disease; it

saps and neutralises all our energy to go out towards mankind
and reach towards that which can include all men.

We must resist making ecumenism into just another
ideology, into a suitable theme for conferences where each
side will persist for centuries in justifying its own position.

We are not denying that there need to be institutions in
which some kind of offering or new approach can be made;
but for us, ecumenism is not an idea, not a notion, but the
response through faith to an event which God has willed in
our history.

In order to achieve our ambition of sharing with modern
man, it is vital that there should be a visible sign of unity in
the entire Christian community. How else can we find the
energy, the joy, the peace, the burning love, all the power and
potential in the Gospels, so as to bring the life of Christ into
the situation of secular man?

What it means to be a 'Catholic'

In our progress towards final reconciliation between all
Christians, the unity Catholics have amongst themselves is
absolutely vital.

Catholics, your very name commits you. Catholic, ecumenical, universal, are all synonymous.

More than ever before, there is a need for solidarity
between all men, all over the world. Without it, there can be
no hope of peace, no hope of human advancement for the
poorest of us. For this reason, the call on you to be faithful to
your name is desperately urgent; to be Catholics is to be open
to everything that concerns man.

And yet, under the very eyes of those who love you, some
of you are at loggerheads.

It is vital that the two sides should meet and come to terms;
this, no one would deny. Each side could come to understand

the attitudes and motives of the other if a dialogue which reached right down to the very depths was opened up.

Such a confrontation calls for clear thinking and a lively examination of the problems, in order to seize on the fundamental principles which create the differences in outlook. Some, in reaction against the great forces of secular culture which surround every Christian, feel that their work should be to emphasise more and more the eternal dimension. Others, though, stress as much as they can the inter-relationships between people.

Tension will become less acute if each side opens its mind to what the Holy Spirit is telling the Church through the voice of others. And dialogue will be even more fruitful if we make an effort to listen carefully to the calls which other Catholics are answering in different kinds of work, but all committed to serving the Christian groups all over the world.

That people should be called different ways is a guarantee of freedom, and also a source of stimulus. Dialogue is made rewarding by this variety. But when the parties who have met lose sight of their objective, when they cease to be preoccupied with men as a whole, they will fall into the temptation of sallying out from behind their barriers only to attack those whose work lies on the other side.

Some of you try to reassure us by saying that no matter how serious the conflict between Catholics, the time for schisms is past; I believe this, too, very deeply, but along with many others, my answer is: In the light of your true vocation which is to be united, surely so much lack of friendship amongst you must eventually fill those who are watching and waiting, with a feeling of indifference?

Catholics, we are waiting for you to turn the hostility, which divides you, into friendship, generously and freely, in full awareness of your universal work, and already, we can sense the joy of that meeting which you will bring us.

DIARY

We must learn how to wait for all these
conflicts to resolve themselves in unity.
This is what I told myself so many times
during the Council.

To find myself in the middle of an
assembly such as that was really a test of
strength, and one for which I felt I had
to prepare myself. All the same, I like to
live on ground-level, amongst men, here at
Taizé, where we have the support of our
community prayer; this I prefer to being
projected into the middle of such an
enormous gathering, even if it is one of
the most fascinating of adventures.

Yes, an adventure! We became more and
more aware of this as the Council drew to
a close, and tension grew with the
increasing importance of the resolutions
taken. And weren't we all, in our human
way, hoping that we would see our own
ideas confirmed in the final documents?

Nothing could have been less ecumenical.
We cannot impose what has not grown and
matured through everyone participating
together; otherwise, we shall only be
subjecting others to our own particular
notions.

For a long time now, the Catholic Church has tried to
preserve its unity by being rather inflexible and very firm.
Was this damaging to the ideal of universal brotherhood?

But this attitude is now changing rapidly. Before, many
barriers were erected; these, modern man has no time for. He

no longer pauses to examine what is behind the barriers he finds. And even if the lines which are drawn are there for the purpose of protecting some value or other which is precious to the Church, they are looked on as an obstacle. Legal definitions impose an unwanted framework; what we need is to find a new language, which can be understood by modern man.

This does not mean that essential elements of our faith must be called into question; simply that to express these same fundamental points in new terms would achieve a broadening of thought which, up to now, has been inconceivable. The unity of the faith would remain protected; the attitude of intransigence would disappear.

But there are some Catholics who are unhappy about the changes which are taking place in their Church which, they say, is 'becoming Protestant' as a result of the Council. For my own part, having attended every session of the Council, I can honestly say that I heard not a single word to suggest that any desire was felt to make the Church of Rome more 'Protestant'.

When, for example, it was decided almost unanimously by the Council to introduce the vernacular into the liturgy of the Eucharist, this was inspired by a concern for universality; this reform, it was hoped, would make the liturgy more accessible to everyone.

Who could be so insensitive as not to appreciate the difficulties faced by all those men and women who were suddenly confronted by changes in the traditional forms of their prayer? It was this prayer which had sustained them since childhood. And yet there is still no case for saying that the Council was trying to 'protestantise' the faith of Catholics. One might just as well claim that it was trying to make their faith Orthodox, since Orthodoxy has always used the vernacular language. Both notions are equally far-fetched.

DIARY

This morning, with some of my brothers, I
attended Sunday Mass at Saint-Germain-des-
près. The church was full, and there were
as many young as old people. The oldest
were sitting on chairs, on three sides of
the altar. Nearly everyone followed the
Mass, in French, in a little book. At the
moment of the consecration, I could see
them whispering the words to themselves -
perhaps a 'concelebration' of an
unofficial kind!

The form of the Mass, kept unchanged over the centuries,
has acquired a great symbolism; it reflects the meaning of
universality. Now, by introducing local languages, it is
hoped to approach closer to every man, the native in the
deepest jungle as much as the citizen of a great capital.

Clearly, these changes create their own problems. Above all,
how can the Eucharist retain a certain surrounding of mystery
which, for men of the technological age, is such a vital
experience? Without it, mankind would veer off course; and
where else but in the Eucharist would men find the presence
of eternity amongst them, daily?

The use of local languages, making the prayer of the Mass
accessible in every country, even on a tribal level, is as much a
feature of universality as the sense of mystery surrounding the
Eucharist. One feature cannot be sacrificed to the other.

And yet there are Christians, today, fighting to impose one
of these features at the expense of the other. Without realising
it, they are reducing the universality of the faith.

For Catholics, there was something of grandeur in possessing
forms of prayer which were centuries old and still unchanged;

now, in order to accept these changes, infinite humility is required. Those Catholics who oppose the reforms and stand up for their 'rights', declaring that they are quite satisfied with things as they are, have turned away from their calling to universality.

In this respect, Protestants, too, must be humble and admit that the fragmentation of Protestant Churches means that there is little recognition between them. There are almost three hundred Protestant denominations; it is hard not to get lost amongst them all!

The use of local languages in prayer has an undeniable value, ecumenically speaking, but we still haven't succeeded, in any of the Churches, in putting it to music.

On the Protestant side, there were composers in the sixteenth century who produced chorale and psalm settings for the prayers, but these settings are now out of date. We do not seem to have any church composers of genius in our day and age. At present, we are forced to carry on using musical settings which are rapidly becoming lifeless. Our experimental age demands new forms which have not yet appeared, but for one or two exceptions.

DIARY

It makes me happy that there is a movement towards the use of local languages; all the same, I know that these in themselves are not enough to destroy an automatic response to the liturgy.

Sometimes, during community prayers, I find myself concerned when the reading from the Bible is given too quickly. I feel a danger that the words can become isolated

like a magic spell, words that 'everyone
should know', and which are never really
understood. People today do not retain
easily what is read to them. Or am I
looking at only half the picture, and
forgetting that many a crumb falls from
the table?

For my own part, I try to meditate on the
epistles of Paul twice a day, and promise
myself to persevere in this study of the
Scriptures.

It is a hard task. Hasn't the Church
always produced some men whose instrument
was the spoken word, and others whose
skill was contemplation? Examined
too closely, the differences between
them seem to be enormous, but seen
at a distance, they reveal one and
the same source of nourishment, of
bread.

Whenever we are confronted with values which the Church
could use to bring Christ to as many men as possible, our
minds appreciate them by conceiving them in a broader,
universal context; in other words, by becoming 'Catholic' in
outlook. When are we going to begin using the phrase 'to be
Catholic' in its full sense, all of us together?

'The Church is called on to renew her Catholic nature continually.'[6]

Who is more aware of his fellow-man than a man or
woman who is truly Catholic? His consciousness refuses
nothing; he notices every human situation; he prays through
the prayer of the centuries offered by the Church, and watches
out for its effects; he weeps for those suffering; he knows the

joy of those whom the day has filled with gratitude. He knows what it is, too, to be passionately devoted to unity, no matter what the cost to him. Not with a dream of unity, but with unity materialised in the institutions of man which, by some sociological law, always tend to become clinkered by local interests and so hinder the power of universality.

Taking the Initiative

While, in some places, ecumenism has made giant strides ahead, there are other places where it is still approached timidly. In some countries, even, there is complete silence on the subject. So that while some Christians have not yet begun the initial, hesitant stages of dialogue, others are well past that stage.

It is important that we should offer concrete possibilities to those who are forging ahead, otherwise we shall find ourselves trapped in a dead-end which will either aggravate the younger generation or drive them into indifference.

Once dialogue has produced a meeting between the two sides, we arrive at the second stage, the stage when action is needed. If we stop short of this stage, we run the risk of satisfying ourselves with a sentimental mood of ecumenism in which it is enough to be aware that there is a separation between Christians and that we must love one another. The young generation look upon this attitude as escapism; they demand realistic action.

While dialogue is actually in progress, the dead-end is not very obvious. But think what disappointment follows when it is finally seen that the relationship which has been formed, for all the meetings it produces, is incapable of uniting the two sides and has only wasted precious time. The honest approach is to admit that dialogue, by itself, lacks the power to create unity. What, then, is the way out of the dead-end?

One step that we can all take and which will bring our objective nearer, is to make unity a reality, to make it come true, all over the world, in individual church communities.

Looking at our past history and the deep parallel ruts we have travelled along to the present day, we can have no illusions at all that unity will come about as a result of decrees or legal bartering. We must simply make unity come true, and, after the event, the Churches which are courageous enough and generous enough will change those forms and structures which no longer correspond to reality.

But to make unity come true, and to adapt oneself to the fact, will require an enormous amount of courage and realism. As for changes in liturgical forms, those will come afterwards. In this respect, the two ancient and mighty Churches, the Catholic and the Orthodox, incur a very large responsibility. They were in existence before the divorce caused by the Reformation. Their power to retain traditions is as great as their power to inaugurate change.

The Eastern Church, with its own difficulties, is also seeking unity; and it can possibly be a source of guidance to us in trying to achieve unity between our own sister-churches.

For ourselves, we are waiting for the moment of reconciliation between our mother Church, the Catholic Church, whose origins preceded the Reformation, and our father Church, the Church which has transmitted the faith of our fathers to us since the Reformation.

As many people realise, there is one person who can perhaps offer us the way out of the dead-end threatening us at present. In the sixteenth century, a Pope issued a condemnation. Today, the Pope has the power to revoke that excommunication which was declared by his predecessor, and to do it without demanding in return that Protestants should renounce their own institutions. Acting as a minister of unity, he will surely have the generosity and greatness of spirit not to demand from other men that they should deny their fathers, who handed down the faith to them with integrity. It would be sad if the Church whose vocation is to be universal and catholic were to show any signs of exclusiveness.

The Pope is in full communion with Eastern Catholics. He does not look upon them as Roman Catholics and, now less than ever, does not ask them to sacrifice their own ways. Why, then, should it be impossible for him to admit as 'Catholics' men and women who are living a faith which is truly universal and ecumenical, and, at the same time, to leave intact the values inspired by the Gospels, which they have inherited?

The Pope is the only man with the power to admit as members of 'the Church' all those who profess the same fundamental faith. To do so would be an act of courage, and it is a gesture which we ask of him with all the daring of peacemakers.

DIARY

In Rome, I was at table with some theologians reputed to be traditionalists, and chatting with them. One of them, the most highly qualified, began to give his opinions about the ways to achieve unity:

If there is a gap between the Catholic and Protestant schools of theology, he said, there are equally wide gaps between the different schools within Catholicism itself. There is as much difference between the Thomists and the Franciscans or Augustinians as there is between Luther and Aquinas. Since the Reformation, though, Catholic theology

has worked in isolation on building up an
ecclesiology, and in defining the rights
and powers of the magisterium so as to
arrive at a rough definition of infalli-
bility.

To hear these words from a theologian
involved in the running of the Catholic
Church, a man who does not see himself
either as a revolutionary or a
relativist, suddenly opened up new per-
spectives.

There is some hope in waiting, then; if
all these different schools submit to
being complementary, they can coexist in
real unity, not only between East and
West, but between all the western Churches
as well.

So that dialogue can move on from its present state, in
which it is faced with a dead-end, there is another decision
which could be taken, which all of us who are close in faith
and share the same prayer, look forward to seeing.

Would it be impossible for the Pope to allow all baptised
Christians who believe in the Real Presence and are seeking
unity, to receive the Eucharist with Catholics? At the same
time, could he take steps to begin a serious study of the
possibilities of intercommunion with those Churches which
would be prepared to co-operate in examining the whole
question together?

The first step would inevitably be clumsy, but the important thing is that it should be taken. How else can we overcome the difficulties which face us? The young generation
have experienced a real taste of ecumenism, and if nothing
concrete emerges, these will become deeply disillusioned.

Ecumenism will be put aside, or else substitutes will be found for a real solution. The *agape* will be adopted as such a practical substitute that the Eucharist will be abandoned and not sought again.

How can we re-emphasise the truth of that old belief that communion 'prefigures' the unity of Christians?[7] If we do not live in one communion, how can we find the strength necessary to create unity?

DIARY

I often think back to the dialogue within myself that I had, as a young man, when I was rediscovering the faith. I found it hard to understand what some people claimed about the Last Supper. For some, Communion was only a meeting in remembrance of Christ. Others saw it just as a meal taken together as brothers.

I had been brought up with the Scriptures since childhood; and I began to think of two sayings of Christ and compare their meaning. The first: 'For where two or three are gathered in my name, there am I in the midst of them'.[8] The second: 'This is my body, this is my blood'. I then decided within myself: whenever I am with other Christians, He is present; He promised so, and I believe His word. But when I take the bread and wine of the Eucharist, I am in a different presence; I am taken into the resurrected Christ. If this is not so, what is the point of the communion meal?

When He says, 'This is my body', Christ is talking about a presence which is different from His spiritual presence among two or three gathered together in His name, as He promised.

To live in the real presence of Christ in the Eucharist is to depend on a faith which cannot come from within ourselves. To reject that faith would perhaps make us more understandable to men, but what meaning would the Gospels have then?

Looking Ahead

Catholics are amazed. Why has there been no greater reception given to the acts of repentance made by their Church towards Protestants?[10]

Already – and the young are loudest in this demand – both sides are called on to make further steps forward.

DIARY

An annoying conversation with someone who wanted to know what special characteristics were found in Protestantism, as opposed to Catholicism. I summoned up all my courage to answer, even though a little voice inside me kept saying: move on to another subject!

What is special about Protestantism? I tried to simplify the question by telling him about ourselves, here. At Taizé there are brothers belonging to twenty different Protestant Churches, as well as the

F

Anglican Communion; that is to say, a community which might well call itself 'ecumenical' rather than 'Protestant', given the presence of Anglicans among us.

Some of our brothers, members of a Protestant Church in Northern Europe, had never seen the Eucharist celebrated facing the congregation before they came to Taizé.

One of us was brought up since early childhood to make the sign of the Cross.

One of us was brought up to go to confession and receive absolution.

Another, again a Protestant, was used to seeing the Eucharist celebrated in the traditional vestments, chasuble, stole, his bishops with a crosier and mitre, candles burning around the crucifix and altar. In his church, hosts were taken at communion, never bread.

And yet another, more exceptionally, was taught by his father, who was a pastor, to honour the Virgin Mary.

Looking at the enormous variety within Protestantism, we can see that all these things belong to it, but none of them are special to it. Where, then, should one draw the line which separates it from others? The crucial difference is, without any doubt, the refusal of Protestants to acknowledge the ministry of the Pope and to accept the modern dogmas concerning the Virgin Mary.

While the reaction of some Christians is to reject all institutions, others are adopting a new approach which is growing more and more widespread; namely, to infiltrate the institutions which will disseminate their ideas and try to guide them towards unity.

Immediately we are confronted by another question. Can the Church, the body of Christ, achieve unity without a visible head? Can we continue our search for unity much longer without accepting the authority of one minister with charge over all other ministers and Christians, and who embodies all the works of mercy in himself?

It would not be realistic to imagine for one moment that the Catholic Church, which accepts such a ministry, will one day abandon it and be without a guide which it has had for centuries and which is in the process of being defined more clearly.

Surely, though, we would all be glad to have the presence among us of one Christian with the strength and power to lead us and be a peacemaker in our name?

But this question demands very deep thought, and I hope to be able to write further about it.

DIARY

When Paul VI took the first step of going to visit the Patriarch Athenagoras, he was using his authority as pope to set a whole relationship in motion again; and when he addressed the Church in Constantinople as a sister-church, with that single phrase he succeeded in freeing ecclesiology from an impossible dead-end.

A thousand years of separation! And then

only three years between the meeting in Jerusalem and the meeting in Constantinople!

The pope is not waiting passively; he is taking the initiative. And yet, if his authority was not recognised, gestures such as these would be fruitless.

This morning, in Rome, I was present at the third meeting, the reception given to the Patriarch Athenagoras in Saint Peter's.

Behind us was a very excited Greek woman, badly placed for a good view of the proceedings, and who gave vent to her feelings in a loud voice: the Patriarch hadn't been given a seat which matched the dignity of his Church!

In front of us, on a large podium, two identical chairs were standing, one for the pope, one for the patriarch. I was glad to see that Paul VI had wanted to place Athenagoras at his side; it was a gesture which would please the Orthodox members of the congregation.

The prayers began, and were followed by addresses. Then, a few minutes later, I saw the silhouette of Paul VI merge into the shadow of the Patriarch.

A thought occurred to me: suppose the Church were to have two heads, for the sake of unity? But this would destroy the image of the body; it would lead to a kind of federalism, not to a true organic unity.

There is yet another area in which we can see new possibilities of progress emerging.

There is one common factor which the Churches of Rome and Constantinople have in their efforts to come together: in their thought, their theology and in the spiritual awareness of their members, the Virgin Mary plays an important role. After four centuries of conspiratorial silence on this subject, how are Protestants going to deal with this fact?

In successive stages over the years, the Virgin Mary has become a subject of conflict; but there was no conflict to begin with.

The Protestants erected their own barriers to protect themselves from what they regarded as. excesses in the Catholic Church.

The Catholics, then, scandalised in their turn by Protestant tendencies which sometimes went too far, increased their attentions towards the mother of Christ. But hasn't their desire to make good the lack of honour paid by Protestants led Catholics to give undue attention to the Virgin Mary?

In this way, a whole chain reaction took place, and the attitudes adopted by one side only managed to intensify feelings on the other side. Theological developments also reflect this process. How can we escape from the vicious circle of opposites which history has trapped us in?

But now there are signs that these attitudes are changing. In the older Protestant Churches, the worst hostility is now restricted to a few extremist circles. Catholics are beginning to ask Protestants: Wasn't the result of your reactions in the past only to make Christ an isolated figure, to present Him to mankind as detached from His Church and detached from all those who have given witness to Him over the centuries? Do you place enough emphasis on communion with the whole body of Christ?

And Protestants, in their turn, ask the Catholic and Orthodox Churches to change the appearance of the very real love that they bear towards the mother of Christ, to make it purer and less encumbered, and to give it the modesty that rightly belongs to it. They would like to see more emphasis placed on the living relationships between Mary and Christ, in a way which will not destroy the reality of their life together on earth, in an obscure town, and amongst poor people.

When we express our veneration by glorifying reality, we make that reality distant and confined. The Gospels do not glorify, for all their light and brilliance, and, for modern man, glory is just a reflection of human grandeur. Whether we like it or not, the more we associate power and effectiveness with things which are only means of reaching God, the more we bring the power and effectiveness of God Himself into doubt.

DIARY

I am always hearing the same question: what changes would you like to see in Protestantism and in Catholicism for the sake of unity?

How can one answer that question without setting oneself up as a judge in one's own right?

But, to begin with, I would like to see the end of that intolerance found in many Protestants under a form of Christianity which creates separations. Protestants have let intolerance grow in them as a means of defence; as a result, they have developed a need for segregation. They have fallen into the temptation of rooting up good wheat along with the weeds,[11] and, quietly and unawares, have become

self-sufficient. Strange as it may seem,
this process can end with a small group
becoming infused with a sense of its own
triumph, as a Reformed pastor pointed out
to me once after a Protestant gathering.
And he was a peaceful and a generous man,
and in no way vindictive.

As for Catholics, I hope that many of
them will lose their desire for power,
even, sometimes, for domination. This
desire can be found in some of the
organisations within the Catholic Church,
as well; far from being a spur to
creativity, it impedes growth.

3

ON THE OTHER SIDE: HOPE

God Penetrates the Impenetrable

FROM THE LARGE-SCALE CONFRONTATION of the Churches now taking place openly, the Church of tomorrow is emerging. A spring season is upon us; we can see small signs of it around us.

Every new birth is accompanied by pain which must be borne patiently. But how can we fail to come through this pain to the other side when we have the encouragement offered by dedicated young Christians?

What is the basis of our hope? It is the mystery of Christ's presence within us.[1] The more deeply a man makes himself aware of that truth, the firmer will his resistance be to the winds and tides agitating the deep and only partially explored depths of the human personality.

This is our hope, the hope which keeps us from abandoning ourselves completely to the waters, the hope which, at the very moment when we are beset by doubts, enters to reassure us that we shall know God, that He is there, further than our poor faith can reach at times.

Every year brings fresh discoveries about the vast hidden areas of the human personality, and still we cannot claim to know them to any great depth. It is these areas which are the source of our actions and our behaviour, but psychological research is still timid in its explanations.

The older a man gets, the more surprised he is to find how little he knows about himself. The further he advances, the more his scant knowledge is brought home to him. Events rarely happen as he would like them to. He discovers that his gifts as a human being are very few. And yet all this can be compensated for by Christ's living presence within him.

For too long we have thought of God as belonging to heights beyond our reach. For it is He who comes to remain deep inside us, where we have never been able to explore, and there, where the threads of our being converge and join, He is, and is the centre-point on which all turns.

DIARY

The number of times I have appealed for unity within us, the unity of our own personal being. By this I mean our own individual reconciliation with God. But I know, too, the struggle which this entails, which goes on from day to day, no matter how old we are. And then, thinking of our own inconsistency and the way we destroy our own progress, I ask myself if we can ever attain such a distant ambition as achieving unity in ourselves.

This unity is given to us momentarily, at times, but, to be honest with myself, I have to admit that when I find myself in that state, I cannot stay long in it. It is a state which we all struggle endlessly

to rediscover; we are continually faced
with beginning the work again, from
scratch, and with creating harmony
between the opposites in us, so that they
become complementary.

If Paul had not written to the
Thessalonians that their faith was
growing abundantly,[2] I would be inclined
to believe that none of us has any hope of
climbing at all, spiritually speaking.

On the other hand, I can easily
understand what Paul means when he says
that their love for others is also
increasing.[3] The more progress a man
makes, the greater his sensitivity towards
others. The man who suffers within himself
on account of himself has a very great
capacity to understand every human
situation.

But can faith itself make progress?
Can it become any easier as, over the
years, it is confirmed by repetition?

But even then, many situations arise
when our faith is surprised and found
wanting. At these moments, don't we wish
we had faith the size of a mustard-seed?[4]

There are many other ways in which we
seem to make no progress at all.

Six years ago we parted with a herd of
cows which we had built up with great
patience over the years. The cows went to
a new co-operative farm which was being
started; here, we even felt glad to be

giving them away, so happy were we to be
sharing our wealth with others.

As time passed, though, the disappear-
ance of the cattle was felt. Because our
involvement in farm-work was cut down,
our life here in the country lost some of
its meaning. Looking after the cows had
been a wonderful way of following the
seasons as they came and went.

There was no longer the irksome burden
of milking-time every morning and night;
in the early years, I used to do all the
milking myself, every day. And then,
there were no longer any new calves to
bring into the world; this is a job one
cannot do with indifference, the moment
of birth has such an atmosphere of
gravity.

It is some years now since we said
goodbye to our cows and they went off to
the collective farm, and yet for all our
gladness at being able to help the farm
when it started, we still feel a certain
emptiness about the milking-sheds at the
side of the house. In this sense, we
have made no progress at all.

To doubt in God's mercy amounts to doubting in God
Himself; by doubting in His mercy, I mean believing that He
forgives, but that there are some faults which cannot be for-
given.

When doubts hide everything from our eyes, a night falls,
and we have to continue believing without anything to cling
to. The only real support left for us is the faith of the Church,

which is not exclusive to a small sanctified élite, but is lived by many Christians to a much greater extent than appears.

These Christians are not surprised to find doubts continually surging inside them; this is no more than human nature. They are more surprised when they find they are able to believe in the Word which has been given to them in the midst of and in spite of, everything. Their faith has nothing to do with logical arguments; it is faith in a simple Word spoken nineteen centuries ago. Much of what they adhered to has been swept away in one tempest after another, and they are surprised, too, to find themselves surviving, although they are only clinging to bare rock.

Faith claims to see without sight.[5] It is not afraid of the dark nor of the dark regions deep in our own selves. It is a certainty which enables us to move onwards in spite of the darkness.

In a sense, prayer, too, is an attitude of doubt towards faith, an active waiting for the moment of understanding when we will perceive the reality of God's creative work in every event in life. Prayer also expresses our wonderment at life and our deep inner gratitude for the gift of life itself.

DIARY

A Protestant friend of mine who has always been deeply committed to his Church, asked me: Must the whole of my life as a Christian be based on myths, on a wager?

I answered: We have to free ourselves from a lot of myths. We are surrounded by men who have given up their faith. For their sake, we must find a new language to express our beliefs, because the old language is boring to those who live their

whole lives in the conviction felt by the
disciples on Holy Saturday, that God is
dead.

As for the suggestion that our faith is
based on a gamble, this has never been
so. We must be careful about the image
we draw up in our own minds of our past
attitudes and motives; once we are a little
distant from them, it is easy for us to
distort them. Doubtless, our motives
were not absolutely pure; we are
imperfect, and remain so.

We do not start from the idea of a
gamble, but - to use newer language to
express our conviction - from the
evidence offered by witnesses whose word
is above suspicion.

As I wrote that, I was thinking of
another friend of mine, an even closer
friend. He is a man who is involved in the
running of organisations and in trade
union work, a man sceptical in
temperament; and yet one day he confided
in me that Christ had visited him. Alone,
and at a time when he least expected it,
he had heard the living Word spoken to
him. How could this man's faith - or my
own, for that matter - possibly be a
gamble?

We mean no exaggeration when we say that, no matter
how pure a man's faith, there are still areas within him which
remain faithless and even pagan in spirit. There is nothing
to be gained from becoming disturbed and worried by this

realisation; yet nor should we accept it and allow these forces in us to hold sway.

Parts of our personality may be inaccessible to us, but to God every part of us is accessible. He enters us without our knowing. He can penetrate what is impenetrable.

This is a certainty we can all cling to. If we reject it in order to live in a blatant state of uncertainty, we expose ourselves to the danger of breaking down, sooner or later. There are some people who actually look for this kind of insecurity, but where does it lead them?

If we persistently think of life as a shifting movement over the surface of hidden, unexplored waters, we create anxiety for ourselves. In addition, we create doubt, because we forget that faith has a wholeness which can touch every fibre of man. We must not become absorbed by the fact that none of us are capable of attaining complete and utter faith; preoccupations like this make us doubt the nature of faith itself. This cannot happen when we look on faith as the certainty that God is invisibly present in every one of us, even when our union with Him is incomplete.

DIARY

Is it showing a lack of respect for psycho-analysis to maintain that we will always have an imperfect knowledge of certain areas within man? I am not well acquainted with the science, but my ideas have been influenced by a conversation I once had with a great enthusiast of psycho-analysis.

His opinion was that it was not a panacea for all ills, and that it should show more humility in its conclusions.

The fact is that analysis itself doesn't automatically produce the desired improvement. Sometimes it can aggravate the disorder which is the source of the trouble.

He believed, too, that neurotic elements - and any other illnesses - which occur in a human being should be used profitably. When the disorder cannot be used creatively, when it is too destructive, then medical treatment takes on its true value. Psycho-analysis is a cure which should be used when everything else has failed.

He reminded me of that age-old doctor, intuition itself, which the Church has always found effective, under the name of spiritual direction. Intuition can perceive all the weaknesses in man which undermine his stability and cause serious mental disturbance, the kind of disturbance which can then become infectious and spread to other people as well.

He spoke to me, too, about many doctors who had made psycho-analysis their speciality. They turned to it with enormous fervour, but never succeeded in subjecting it to a regular discipline. In no time at all, they saw themselves as the wise men of the century. In their hands, they claimed, were the keys to all knowledge. But in fact, they were going from one disaster to another.

The modesty which I found in this particular doctor was enough to give me confidence in the serious possibilities of psycho-analysis. For him, the subject had not assumed the proportions of a system nor had it elevated itself into a philosophy.

How can we open up the depths of our personality to Christ? How can we give Him access to us? By telling Him everything about ourselves. By examining, in His presence, all those preoccupations which fill our minds. By describing, when we speak to Him, the various things we find oppressive. By showing Him, openly, the difficulties which obstruct us, which come from the depths of ourselves. And, over the years, by coming to be aware of all the hidden values within ourselves, which otherwise would have remained unused.

In the course of this prayer, we hear the answers which are made to us. The dialogue continues, in spite of all the slowness and in spite of moments when the task seems impossible. Then, one day, we reach the very centre of ourselves. Everything comes within our grasp, without difficulty, not only our own sources of inner conflict, but also the conflict inside those who attack us and condemn us.

By being aggressive with himself, man discovers a presence in himself: Christ within him.[6] Only the aggressive in spirit can achieve this.[7]

Our true nature can be born if we struggle to reject everything in us that is ambiguous. Whatever value comes of this in other ways, it has the one point in its favour that it makes us refuse to conceal anything from God when we are praying.

You may argue at this juncture that God can see everything. That is true, but man is always tempted to find ways round the truth in this respect, as though he were keen to preserve a part of himself in complete privacy. But those who do this create friction in their relationship with God, in the same way that two people who are close can create friction when one of them tries to hide something which the other can deduce quite easily from the evidence available.

Christ within us! We can scarcely believe it possible, so much are we aware of our guilt as human beings.

But too often we let the Jansenist attitude come to the fore, when we say: Lord, I am not worthy that you should enter under my roof.[8]

The presence of another within me! I discover this presence when I pray, when I seem to abandon my own being, my own body, in order to understand and grasp Christ in me.

The presence of another within me! One who can harness the weaknesses and contradictions in me. I begin to understand the real meaning of trials and difficulties, for He is the outcome, the sole outcome, of all my suffering. There can be no fulfilment without undergoing trials.

DIARY

We have come to spend a few days with some brothers in a house which has a terrace overlooking the sea.

What could be better. Here, the air is always fresh, a breeze blows in from the sea, the scent of flowers is all around; we enjoy the bright morning light and the cool of the evening following the heat of the day.

In the evening, I cannot resist retiring quietly for a short time and going out on to the western terrace, where there are two orange trees growing.

G

This is a time for thinking. This evening I realise that the last two years have made time seem heavy. They have been full of moments when I have felt that the effort necessary to persevere is too great; and yet whatever has to be done, I succeed in doing it. But I didn't get that feeling during my first twenty-five years at Taizé.

There is one thing I am convinced of: this immense struggle we must fight is a struggle against the powers of darkness which are at work.[9] These powers do not want there to be visible unity, and they know the suffering felt by Christ as He watches His Church being broken and divided.

And so I have accepted the fact that the struggle could be even worse.

This makes me feel at peace; but still I have to overcome my own weariness. I have to keep myself at work so as to be ready to withstand the greatest difficulties when they come.[10] I can do only one thing, abandon myself to Christ. I must call Him whenever I need Him, and I must be aware all the time that He is near at hand.

As I had dinner, it seemed to me that everything was full of light. No one knew it, but I was a rich man, rich with the friendship of Christ and with the friendship of my brothers.

What has been known as 'spiritual direction' is also a way of revealing one's whole self, but in the presence of another man.

Who can truly say, 'There is nothing hidden in me that I haven't admitted either in confession or in intimacy?' Who can say, 'I know everything about myself, I know what it is to see right into the depths of my being.' Only a very few can make that claim. To achieve this, we must place ourselves under Christ's direction; and it takes many years to achieve a clear vision of ourselves.

But when we have that vision, the whole of the body shares in it.[11] The whole being, the body too, is given health when our eyes are clear and fresh and when our spiritual life is full of light. The body – which we have to take into account all the time, which we have to drag along sometimes – is what contains our inner life. The body bears Christ Himself, and the light of Christ fills the body when our being has discarded all that is false and has submitted itself to persevering in the work of exposing every facet of ourselves to Christ.

Those who return to this work day after day can come to know hours of peace and hours of joy.

We throw off that persistent feeling of being ashamed to be alive. This is a feeling which can do damage in many ways; it can prevent us from communicating deeply with anyone and it also saps our energies. It is a form of suffering which has no profit to show for it. Sometimes, by a contradiction in its outlook, Christianity appears to encourage this shame of being alive; Christianity, more than anything else, can saturate us with guilt.

When we have achieved this clearness within us, our failures, obstacles and incapacity, are all seen in a new light.

Anguish itself, which is the source of many an inner force in us – anger, love, harshness and tenderness – is also brought into harmony. Anguish is like a belt of thick mist which we have to cross; we must face it and go through it, rather than go round, and then we find that anguish contains its own solution.

And the more this inner clearness grows, the more we spread peace around us.

DIARY

Every day brings its own struggle; this is known to everyone who has taken on a commitment. Without this struggle, there would be no progress. All through our life our capacity for being strong and decisive needs to be continually renewed. This is true for all of us. The strength of our will-power is for ever being reforged, and yet the resources in us for doing so are unending, to a degree we could never begin to realise.

Often in my mind, I think about all the opportunities lost; I think about all the places where it would have been good to set up the Community when we started, and I compare them inwardly with the province of Mâcon, where we finally settled; a province which is poor, in the ordinary human sense, and completely dead, from the point of view of the Church.

But to live in the past or in the future is useless. The imagination only creates dramas for itself. Today is all that matters. Of course we cannot live without having an eye to the future, but it is fatal to become absorbed in speculation.

When we allow Christ to penetrate the impenetrable, we are tirelessly trying to recover the state of childhood. This does not prevent us from being or becoming mature as men; there is nothing 'childish' about being a child in this sense.

It means to be oneself, without adopting poses and being superficially adept. Nothing is more harmful to communion and nothing is so destructive to integrity as wearing a mask which is not true to ourselves.

DIARY

A priest whom I have never met wrote me a letter which I pinned up on the wall of my room. It has been there for many years now; every now and again I stop to read it:

'Today I celebrate the tenth anniversary of my ordination. I could not help thinking of you and your community. Together, we are all trying to scale the same mountain, though by different paths, towards Christ.

'I remembered a little short-cut which perhaps will help us to be together a little sooner. This short-cut is for us to be children in spirit.

'I firmly believe that this is the way we shall achieve unity. The final union will take place in an atmosphere of childhood, with humility, simplicity, confidence, and complete trust.

'This path, this way, I would like humbly and simply to bring to your notice, today.'

Friendship – the Presence of God

The deeper a man's knowledge of himself, the more he realises that he will die knowing no more than the shape and form of his own personality as it moves over the vast hidden waters of the unconscious. And yet, out of these waters emerge a few rocks firm enough for him to build on.

One of these rocks is confidence, confidence placed in another person.

When this confidence takes the form of friendship, our sense of security grows; it becomes possible for us to begin work in common, to build together, not for oneself but for others, in a way which results inevitably from friendship.

We have to know the meaning of solitude before we can understand the true value of certain kinds of human contact.

Lasting friendship for life is not granted to everyone. But periods of deep friendship, experienced and passed through, can recur over a whole lifetime. Each experience of this kind reawakens a living spirit which we would not know but for friendship, and this spirit moves in our very depths, transforms us, makes us human, and revives in us a comforting awareness of the welcome one man can extend to another.

DIARY

On the subject of friendship, I wrote these words to one of my brothers:

'Friendship is a value which we shall never understand in depth; we shall only come to know its rough outlines, and touch on its depths only for brief moments.

'Friendship inspires dialogue in which we feel able to confide calmly in others, and by doing so, discover - not everything about ourselves - but many facets of ourselves. In this way, it brings something to life in us; it is as though it were a bringing forth of Christ.'

And one of my brothers wrote to me:

'At times when God seems to be testing our friendship for Him, our friendship towards other men and towards our brothers takes on a new dimension, a dimension of eternity.'

Through friendship, we can sense the existence of an invisible world; nothing else displays so luminously the face of God on earth.

Faith does not proceed from friendship, but can be sustained by it. Since the appearance of the very first Christian communities, a chain of friendship has linked man to man; this makes us realise that it is not my personal faith which counts, but the faith of the Church together.

From the very beginning the cry has been the same: 'Look not upon my sins' – upon my lack of faith – 'but on the faith of your Church.'[12]

DIARY

A few notes taken during the sermon given by an Anglican bishop in our church:

'We talk too much about love, and men do not understand. They would understand better if we talked about friendship.

'Friendship means confiding in others. In religious terms, we call this faith.

'Friendship also means conversation with others. In religious terms, we call this prayer.

'Friendship is expressed through gestures, like shaking hands, embracing. These things are signs of friendship. In religious terms, we call these sacra-ments.'

The bishop ended by saying: 'Friendship of any kind always contains an element of adoration.'

Our thirsting after intimacy with others surely stems from our foreknowledge of another, deeper communion, which we shall have with Christ Himself.

The modern generation is more preoccupied with com-munication than ever before. Perhaps men are now ready to understand how, at a given moment, one single Person might be able to conquer our solitude in a way in which no ordinary human intimacy can.

When a man is dominated by a passionate desire for friendship, he feels emotional needs which are often out of proportion to the real relationship. He becomes the victim of an illusion which, if he does not succeed in dispelling it, can cause the other to put up barriers in self-defence, to turn away and renounce the friendship. In this case, friendship has come to be a means for self-satisfaction, giving nothing freely. There is no friendship in a relationship which holds either person captive. Without sacrifice, which purifies, there can be no friendship.

DIARY

This evening, some young people were asking me the meaning of giving freely.

Giving freely is the way in which man shows he will not hold another in captivity.

Giving freely means advancing, advancing over our own bodies, as one might say in the language of the epics. And this advance leads us towards communion which, once attained, reveals life to us in a way which cannot be compared to anything else.

And when we open ourselves in friendship to non-believers, additional benefits can come of our relationship.

In these modern times when society is becoming more and more secular and man is turning away from our ancient creed of Christianity, we are often approached by men and women, self-professed atheists, who are generously looking for contact with us. Some of these no longer condemn us; they are now interested in dialogue with us; and for our part, starting a dialogue with them can make us more human. The truth is – and this is something we have to be very tactful in revealing – some people, without knowing why, are struck by the mystery of life; these are the believers. Others, without denying this mystery, do not commit themselves; these are the agnostics. And then there are the atheists who refuse to accept that there is any mystery at all. And then 'how ironical it is that secular society can produce forces of unity and recon- ciliation which often seem more catholic than the forces we see operating in the Church'.[13]

DIARY

I have never had so much dialogue with agnostics as I have over the last few years. Only yesterday, an agnostic writer

– whom I still haven't met – sent me a copy of his latest book and a note saying, 'Hoping that an agnostic will find a welcome at your open doors.'

A few days ago, in the middle of the group sessions which we hold here continually, two young students from the neighbourhood, neither of them baptised, came to tell us about their forthcoming marriage. They said they did not want a blessing; it would be against their conscience. The girl belongs to a family in which no one has been baptised for generations, perhaps since the revolution. The boy, too, is from a non-Christian family. But they feel that their day of joy, their wedding-day, should be marked by some sort of celebration. Why not bring the two families together in an act of sharing? And so, in the evening, after the wedding, I met the two old-established families on the gallery of the church (which overlooks the whole of the interior).

We talked simply. Dialogue was possible because one man, John XXIII, has removed the barriers which were there before. We were all aware of this fact.

The bells rang for prayer. I went to my place and, as the evening prayers were said, I knew that they were still standing there in the darkness of the church, although they had never been baptised.

Towards a New Society

We tend to forget that we have now entered the new age of atomic power. The very survival of the human race depends on harmony being established between all men. Will Christians be the first to settle their differences and so begin a movement towards unity between men everywhere?

In the present age, the old ethnic structures are crumbling. There is relative peace to a certain degree, but it is dependent on a balance of aggressive power and not on international understanding. Atomic weapons are capable of destroying the whole earth.

DIARY

These last years of our lives have been overshadowed by a prolonged war being fought in Vietnam. It was striking for us here at Taizé to hear a Vietnamese who had visited us say the following words at our night prayer:
I am afraid of my fear,
I am afraid of abandoning you, Lord,
I am afraid of my fear,
I am afraid of not enduring to the end.
Do not forget that I live for you.
Allow me to give you my whole life
Together with the love which will make me one with you.

If we are trying to prepare the way for peace, surely we must concentrate on the ways in which we can prevent wars from beginning.

By praying for the development of deprived countries and by working together for human progress, we can make up for some of the injustice in this world and, at the same time, create conditions in which peace can emerge. Today, peace means progress for all; the two are inseparable.

Christians in the world are struggling for peace with tremendous generosity; yet we have to admit that they find it difficult to halt conflicts once these have started. Even when Pope Paul VI, bravely and with all his spiritual authority, appealed to these engaged in war, saying 'Stop, in the name of Christ!' it was a long time before peace negotiations began.

The way to peace has to be prepared while there is time, before things become too bad, and the development of the underprivileged nations is one of the first requirements. If we ignore this necessity, we shall be condemning those nations to the only path open to them, the path of armed conflict.

Many Christians in wealthy countries take the trouble to imagine for themselves what it must be like to live through a famine; generously, they give up some of their possessions in order to help. Aggressively, like true peacemakers, they try to wake the conscience of Christians and non-Christians around them to the problem. They are putting into practice what was demanded of Christians fifteen centuries ago when capitalism was appearing in an early form: 'It is because some men try to appropriate for themselves possessions, which are common to all, that conflicts and wars break out amongst men, as though nature itself were up in arms at the fact that man, with those cold possessive words – "yours" and "mine" – was creating a separation where God had instituted unity . . . The possessions in your trust are the possessions of the poor, whether you have earned them by a lifetime of honest work or by inheritance.'[14]

Yet, what can we effectively do? The gestures we make to help the Third World, the money we collect, are but small indications of what must be done.

For a serious start to be made in developing the countries of the Third World, the rich nations would have to contribute one per cent of their national revenue. But instead of a contribution on this scale, all we see is a drop in the amount of aid given to underdeveloped countries.

Population growth in poor countries increases at such a rate that, now, if affluent societies were to share out their own produce, there would not be enough to go around. It is in the poor countries themselves, on the spot, that these problems will be solved, given technical guidance from the more advanced nations.

DIARY

A conversation with an economist, who was assuring me that the day was fast approaching when technical means of production would abolish starvation from the face of the earth.

The responsibility he bears in his job can be seen in his face. He made me reflect on the fact that, in co-operation with others, we are trying to find ways of helping the poor nations to emerge from their present difficulties.

Our thoughts on the subject may or may not be of value, but it seems to us that there are two steps in approaching the problem. The first is to make all men aware of their human nature. The second is to teach them how to survive.

To achieve these ends, we must educate people. The ignorance of the masses in rural communities of the southern hemisphere either makes them the victims of oppression today or will do in the future;

in addition, it means that they do not use
the best methods available for cultivating
their land.

Without a minimum of knowledge, we
cannot come to know ourselves as
human beings; nor can we learn how to
support our bodies properly.

The most effective way we can achieve
these two vital stages towards progress is
through the means we have of transmitting
television by satellite. The same television image can reach enormous areas of
different languages and dialects, and
could be accompanied by commentaries in all
these languages, transmitted by satellite
on different channels.

Techniques like these have arrived in
time to compensate for the lack of
facilities available for education; they
are also inexpensive to use. A series of
ten transmissions would be enough to cover
all the countries of the Third World, at
an expense of about four hundred million
dollars.

In this way, the most isolated village
would be able to receive daily an
educational programme and each member
of the village learn from it what he
needed for himself. The inhabitants of
those countries which are developing
would learn, on a vast scale, how to
plant crops, work the land and reap the
best harvest.

This would have the added benefit of

reducing the continual migration of rural
population to the inhuman areas surrounding
the great cities.

When the latest chemical methods –
which rely on petroleum-based fertilisers
– are employed in producing the crops for
animal foodstuffs and, later, crops for
human consumption, the day will come when
all will share in the riches of the land.

The living conditions of so many people
could be changed by an educational
programme of this kind. Those who have
suffered injustice and fear for thousands
of years will be reached by a network of
audio-visual communication and will learn
the benefits to be had from human
scientific knowledge.

The way in which the races complement
one another has also led to a form of
dialogue.

Once the poorest races have become aware
of their full humanity, this too will
make us all understand the vital way in
which northerners and southerners complement one another.

Races in the southern hemisphere have
an amazing gift of perception through
which they see exterior reality with an
intensity and intuitive grasp which others
lack.

Men in more temperate or cold climates
tend to apply intellectual analysis to
situations. In some respects, they are

poorly equipped in contrast with black
people or Indians who possess such a rich
faculty of perception.

The races of the southern hemisphere
have an artistic and creative capacity
which represents a real force in the
world, and which could well come to the
aid of northern civilisation with its
intellectual atrophy. For the north and
the south to be separated would mean
death for the human race. Our hope for the
future lies in the complementary character
of our different cultures, and the creative
interaction which can take place between
the intuitive gifts of the one and the
analytical gifts of the other.

Perhaps western civilisation will overcome the difficulty it finds in
establishing true human communion by
allowing itself to be influenced by the
spontaneity which we associate above all
with black people. Black communities work
together creatively, as a group. We, on
the other hand, tend to live as individuals, a tendency which has been
reinforced by the affluence of our
societies. Could our individualism learn
how to share from being in contact with
southern cultures? If we never acquire a
capacity for sharing, we cannot hope that
wealthy societies will ever become
generous and open-handed.

The southern races, then, can teach us
the meaning of working creatively

together. An economist to whom I made
this point replied that this is precisely
what industrial production needs for it to
contribute successfully to the good of all.

He believed that expansion of the most
important industries will depend, not on
more capital - which the State or
private sources can easily supply - but
on building up united working teams with
intelligent and experienced staff. The
time has passed when an individual, on his
own, could direct the growth of a
business. Now, business needs teams of
technicians of the first order. It will
advance to the stage where it will be able
to finance itself and, without needing
resources from outside, its pace of growth
will increase yearly through its own
momentum.

Industry of the future will not need
investments from outside, for it will
itself supply the funds necessary for its
growth. What will matter above all will be
the competence of its workers, their
team spirit and their creative work
together.

And so the people of the poorest races,
by their understanding of creative co-
operation, will possibly be an active
force in our future development.

With every year, the relationship between the consumer
societies of capitalist countries and the industrial societies of
Eastern Europe becomes closer and closer. They have one

H

factor in common: all industrialised countries base their economy on the needs of the consumer. The arrival of the computer is speeding up this process which is binding countries more closely together.[15]

If the sole object of progress were to make our societies into societies of surplus production, man would reach the stage where there would not be enough leisure facilities to distract him from boredom and despair.

We can avoid becoming spiritually stifled in this way by creating a new society based on participation, on sharing in common.

But this new society, as well, would be provisional, a means of progressing to a further stage. Once poverty has been abolished and men in every country are living in equally good conditions, what will be the point of human existence? What use will man make of his creative power, which delights in seeking challenges?

Material possessions, by freeing men and women from irksome burdens, are a source of great good; but they are not an end in themselves.

Christians, together with non-believers, must examine seriously what the following stages are to be, stages which, in their turn, will be provisional.

In every country, men are forming groups and looking together at these questions, so as to be in tune with the forces governing society both now and in the future. In addition to these study groups, other groups are taking concrete action, forming the pattern of our future society: in agriculture, we find communal farms, and in the cities, worker groups which are dedicated to social problems.

Do we find Christians who are afraid of getting involved in the work of human progress for fear of dirtying their hands? Yes, Christian piety has a bad name for the way it has prevented men from pursuing human knowledge, economics and politics. And yet accepting God's will means more than just saying, 'Lord, Lord';[16] it means fighting courageously for the good of men.[17]

Over the years to come, true Christians will be recognised by their contribution to a new Christian attitude towards society. For the layman, this will mean committing himself to 'politics' in the broadest sense of the word; not fighting a party battle within narrow horizons, where one can easily end up struggling for the interests of a small group of people, but materialising the ambition of building the human city.

This new Christian attitude is vital if we are to have any influence over large-scale social changes. To give an example of this: if the profound transformation affecting the countries of Latin America takes place without the participation of Christians, this would mean the end of the Church in those countries. And if the Church were to collapse in Latin America, Christianity would be confined to the northern hemisphere. How could Christians then profess that their vocation is to be catholic, to be ecumenical?

Men everywhere are bound, in one way or another, by this necessity, the necessity for working for the common good of all. This is not something which can be reduced to a limited area of society, on a local level or on a national level. The Christian, when he has fought to make himself aware of the needs of men everywhere, will be called on more and more to share his possessions among the rest of men; and this is the way that a society based on human participation and human sharing will be formed in the future.

When we are working for the future of society by opening our minds to all men's needs, we can become involved in human interests which are complex and even contradictory. How can we guard against the danger of being swamped by all these calls on our attention, or sinking hopelessly in a mass of human passions of all kinds? Surely we shall have to watch where we tread, because of the risk that every fresh step we take may trap us inescapably? On the other hand, though, how can we refuse to commit ourselves, no matter how often?

Christians must take all the responsibility for whether the new society is built with their help, or without it. Even so, some Christians create tension because, in their extreme enthusiasm, they want to impose a solution on social problems in an exclusively 'Christian' sense. Only if we all realise that our commitment as Christians or as non-Christians is complementary will this tension disappear.

Generosity is made ineffective by quarrelling amongst ourselves. Those of us who are concerned with the situation in the world and want to help find an answer are only divided by intolerance and condemnation. It is useful to remember that the kind of intolerance which has characterised the past history of some countries has made them sometimes use oppressive measures like those of the Inquisition.

We need to accept that man's problems can be approached in many different ways if the tensions of the present are going to give way to tensions of a better kind. Some of us will direct our spirit in such a way that it will be a hidden presence among the poor people of the world. Others, on the other hand, will work actively in the field. And others will apply themselves to thought and deep reflection aimed at destroying tyranny among men. All these different ways together will contribute to building the new society.

DIARY

I was talking to a brother who is about to
leave for one of our open communities,
and we were asking ourselves the question:

'What meaning will our life as religious
have in man's future?' We shall be the
living Word in a world full of injustice
and intolerance; we shall be a prayer
offered up through an absurd way of life
which reason can't justify; we shall be
the language of men spoken to God every
time we show love to the afflicted; and
our life will be a page in the life of
men inscribed with all the sufferings
endured for His Body, which is the
Church.[18]

Recently, a religious wrote to us com-
plaining about one of our communities,
saying that our brothers refused to agree
with him on a certain issue. The man who
wrote is an intellectual and writes well.
He wanted us to express ourselves in
writing as well, and said that we would
show ourselves to be deeply committed if
we would oppose the signing of a particular document. Committed to what,
exactly, we wanted to know ... A few months
later his attitude changed completely.

There is a form of commitment which
counts for more than signing petitions
and writing articles, no matter how just
the cause: it is to endure daily the
hardships of a life unrelieved by
distraction, and to share fully in the life
of men and women who have abandoned all
hope of better conditions.

I agree that some written declarations
in the past have produced an effect and

were a valid form of commitment for those who inspired them, but, all I can say is that, in our time, there are too many petitions, too many men called on to sign this or that appeal, for or against.

Is it not more effective to be men who are ready to listen? This attitude has never prevented men from becoming involved in the life of others. Some of my brothers have worked, or are working now, as common labourers; some live amongst the poorest of people. Their presence in itself is a declaration. No written formula is necessary. Very often those who commit themselves through written statements fail to do so in any other concrete way. Very often the written word is just a means of quietening our conscience.

When our meetings with others have to be rounded off with written resolutions of a praiseworthy kind, one side or the other may well be forced to be hypocritical. Nowadays we declare our support in writing; we declare our opposition in writing; we shelve an issue in writing; all this changes not a jot our actual way of life. The whole process is becoming one of the weaknesses of our time.

I asked the organisers of a large Christian Peace Movement in what way we could help them, and their only answer was: Sign letters, sign petitions.

In our fight for peace, the intermingling of races will eradicate one source of conflict in the world.

In Brazil this has taken place quite successfully. Over the generations, a race of mixed blood has grown up, a society open to all and rich in creative art. But in the United States, the present crisis is due to the fact that intermingling has been forbidden by society.

DIARY

I have received two letters from brothers abroad, which arrived almost together. One is from Brazil, the other from the United States. What they say is very significant.

First, the letter from Recife: 'Our life with people here who are, along with the Indians, among the poorest in the country, has moments of rewarding fullness. We are struck by the suffering and ill-feeling caused by unemployment – but then we are not welcomed very openly in the factories because of our European nationality and background – yet this is compensated for by the enormous hospitality shown to us. A family is quite likely to give a stranger all the food there is in the home, even if they will have to go hungry themselves for a few days.

'As a result of racial mixing, art is very rich in expression here in Brazil. The "bossa nova" in poetry, singing and literature is something which has a universal appeal; for western countries it will have an impact similar to jazz, which the Africans gave them.'

The letter from Chicago: 'Our black friends around us here where we live are slowly becoming more distant towards the liberal whites. Three out of four black pastors among our friends say to us: "We want power for the black people. Why don't you go and teach white people whatever it is you want?"

'And then, there are many young people who ask: "Where can we find hope?" I don't know what to say except: In the resurrected Christ.

'Here in our community, now that our friendship is refused by some, what else can we do except go down on our knees and pray, saying: "Christ, have pity on us all, because we are white."'

There are, in fact, two black men living in the community and sharing in their troubles.

Accompanying the letter came a photo clipped from a newspaper, showing a fight between black, white and yellow men which took place in the street where our brothers live.

We had a visit from a black bishop from the west coast of Africa; his origins are the same as those of the Negro people in the United States who are the descendants of slaves shipped to America. We talked together about the situation there.

His face was very calm and open; the face of an extremely sensitive man, showing very clearly how much he had suffered. I wanted to know why, and then, talking to him, I discovered the anguish he felt for his fellow-Negroes in America.

What contradictions there are amongst men! In the United States, the black people who have suffered patiently for so long have now erupted in revolt. At the same time, in his diocese in Africa, this bishop can see young Americans who have gone there to work. They are loved by the black people. They live in the poorest parts and the spirit they show is the spirit of humanity.

But when they go back home, what will they find? They will find that 'the central quality in the Negro's life is pain - pain so old and so deep that it shows in almost every moment of his existence ... The Negro while laughing sheds invisible tears that no hand can wipe away'.[19]

Violent for Peace

There are many young people, Christians and otherwise, who want to revolutionise present social structures by definite action of some sort; they believe that only violence will achieve this end. Some of them know, too that only the aggressive in spirit will possess the kingdom of God.[7] The faint-hearted, the apathetic, those who do not know what it is to feel the spur of passion, all these, because of their very nature, will not discover the kingdom. Christ also said: Blessed are the peace-makers. [20]

The aggression of the peacemaker! The whole spirit of the Gospels – a spirit which can cause revolution on earth – is perhaps summed up in that apparent contradiction.

But we must not deceive ourselves. Not any violence will do. The aggression which will possess the kingdom is creative aggression. There is no desire for power behind it.

In the name of Christ, men have fought with the wrath of the crusades, they have subjected others to their own convictions, encouraged sectarianism and revolt, wedged themselves behind 'purist' attitudes of one kind or another. Throughout history, men have killed one another in Christ's name. Many, by their writings alone, have brought shame on humanity. Destructive aggression amongst Christians – with rebellion on the one hand and counter-attack by traditionalists on the other – has meant a tremendous collapse in the structure of God's Church.

Whenever we spark off destructive aggression between Christians, surely we are crucifying the body of Christ in the name of so-called lofty causes? Far from bringing us into the kingdom, conflict of this sort makes us unfit to enter. [21]

Here at Taizé, sixteen hundred young people who had come together declared themselves to be 'aggressive, yes, but not in revolt'. They added: 'We are not in revolt, and we ask nothing for ourselves. But, with the aggression of peacemakers, we appeal on behalf of those who are not members of the Church, those on whom we look, not with impatience, but quite the reverse. And yet our patience is accompanied by suffering when we see the young men and women for whom we are trying to live in Christ displaying indifference towards the faith. Some of them have known what it is to love the Church and to hope deeply in the Church, but they have not stayed. They have crept away from us. And others who have been brought up amongst indifference, cannot see in separated Christians the sign of brotherhood and community which all men are looking for.'

We have often felt, over the last two years, during these large international gatherings of young people at Taizé, that the vitality of the younger generation would soon burst the banks of their patience; amongst the older generation, too many have rejected coldly what has been growing in the awareness of the young.

DIARY

I was talking to a group of about twenty young people from West Berlin. They were brought up as Protestants, but quite openly admit the fact that they are sceptical about all church institutions. They are interested only in violence. The memory is vivid in their minds of one of their number who was killed by the police during a demonstration.

They asked me: 'Why doesn't your community use the newspapers to spread its ideas? You are well known in Germany and you could do a lot. Why don't you yourself as prior of the community, speak your mind publicly more often?' We had the following exchange; first I answered:

- Here, as brothers, we all complement one another, myself as much the rest of my brothers.

- Yet you are in a position to speak. You don't realise what an audience you have.

– What counts in a man is his inner
self. The exterior image which others have
of me matters little to me. The inner self
of a man prefers to live a certain
amount in silence, and doesn't believe
very strongly in making declarations.

– You should write to the President of
the United States.

– I already have, and I have no
illusions about the effect my letter will
achieve. Anyway, many people have
intervened like this, and still the war is
being fought.

– Then violence is the only thing that
shows dividends.

– Violence can be used only when all the
means of passive resistance and all the
means of persuasion have been tried. No
man may decide to use the extreme measure
of violence unless he does so in a spirit
which is totally free of personal
interests. And we must remember, too, that
the man who takes up a sword to strike
another will perish by the sword.[22]

I advised them to read, that very
evening, a passage from a recent writing
on 'the advancement of all races' which is
most rewarding. I pointed out especially
that, here, for the first time, a pope,
after warning us against temptations to be
violent, allows for the fact that, in
exceptional circumstances, violence can
justifiably break out. This can happen, he
writes, 'when men are subjected to clear

and prolonged tyranny which could
constitute a grave threat to basic
human rights and seriously harm the
common good of a country'.[23]

But why have these young people come here
to pose questions to me? As far as they
are concerned, ecumenism doesn't exist.
To them, there is no difference between
Protestant and Catholic. As regards faith,
they have no idea where they stand.
Therefore we were all the more surprised
to see them take communion at our daily
eucharist.

Back in my room, alone, it seems to me
that I cannot let them leave here without
listening to them again. Violence has a
prophetic value of its own; I cannot shut
my ears to it. I remember, too, that
Christ, dying on the cross, promised
eternal life to a man who lived by
aggression.[24]

Yesterday I invited them to breakfast
in the house. I noticed the cold look in
the eyes of one of them, a young girl, a
look full of hostility. She had enough
strength of character to create a common
feeling of aggression around here, a feeling of adherence to violence as a
necessary thing. If a psychiatrist had
seen them, he would have diagnosed this
feeling as a group psychosis. True, some
of the prophets in Israel were far from
mentally balanced. But these youngsters,
fortunately, like myself, have had to

contend with passionate arguments flung in their faces by others, and so they have thought and re-thought their attitude and given them a fair appearance of validity.

They find the war in Vietnam intolerable. They want to act against it. I told them: for my own part, I would like one of my brothers to go to Vietnam with a young American who is staying here at the moment, who came back from Vietnam wounded very deeply in spirit. But as for you, what can you do? Shouldn't you go to Vietnam as well?

The girl whose force of character animated the whole group got around to talking about Latin America, saying that a revolution is necessary there to free the poor. More Vietnams are needed in the world, in Christian society as much as in other kinds of society.

I said then that perhaps participating together in the work of progress can resolve our problems without our having recourse to bloodshed and insurrection. Women and children don't particularly want to be the victims of these uprisings.

What matters to you above all is committing yourselves, whether in the Third World or here in the heart of your own society. Finish your studies, then, as quickly as you can; we need a certain amount of education before we can start.

Once you have committed yourselves, perhaps some of you will one day oppose

in all conscience a source of clear and
prolonged tyranny that you come up
against, tyranny which oppresses humanity
and shows no respect for life. Even then,
you will still need to examine your
motives deeply, because the temptation
to be violent haunts us all through
our life. When we believe we must destroy
in order to create, our first duty is to
look into ourselves and find our motives.

By identifying violence with destruction, aren't you turning yourselves into a
sect which is pursuing an idea on its
own? Isn't this what we see in those who
harbour the secret desire to become
political leaders? Their arguments may
sound idealistic, but their motives never
are. They have no real urge to give freely
and even less urge to forget their own
interests.

Destructive aggression can set in motion
waves of increasing violence. The
liberals who go along with it, to start
with are usually eliminated or executed
in the second or third wave, because they
refuse to accept destruction as an end in
itself.

I know that in Latin America, the
symbol of the cross is the symbol used
by some who are Christians only in name;
we see the poor treated with contempt by
them, power grasped and wielded. All this
is violent aggression disguised as
something else, and what an image it gives

of the Church! Newspapers and television spread this image to us here in Europe.

Using money to satisfy a need for power is another form of tyranny, though tyranny itself does not need money behind it. There are police regimes in parts of the world where capitalism has crumbled or disappeared, and what oppression we see in these places!

Tyranny can even present itself as inspired by the most humanitarian ideals, and cloak under elevated ideological principles the wretched servitude to which it subjects people.

Yesterday, it was the Berliners. Today, in spite of the fact that it is mid-winter and we are in an isolated part of the country, once again I am confronted by people with similar ideas. Some young people arrived here; they are from another European country, and they ask me the same questions. As soon as I met them, I could sense a bitterness in them which I hadn't found in the young Berliners.

Briefly speaking, they asked me this: Why do you refuse to do away with church institutions? You should be trying to sweep the board clear. Without violence, you won't convince the hierarchy of anything. We would prefer your community not to exist at all if you don't look at things in this way.

I tried to understand them. In the

conversation which followed, I can
remember telling them: why do you want to
use your young energies in destroying?
Why don't you go and build up small
communities or brotherhoods, starting in
some small country village somewhere, a
village which has its own unity and where
life hasn't disappeared? Coming face to
face with the people of the village -
some of them agnostics - will force you to
shrug off everything in your idea of a
vocation which isn't evangelical in
spirit. Since they will react slowly to
you, being country-folk, you will have
time to step back and look at the problems
more clearly, and then, after gaining that
first experience, you can go on to
approach the masses. If there were an
older man amongst your number, you would
represent all the better - like a
microcosm - the world-wide human
community which is made up of all the
generations.

As regards the ancient institutions of
your Church, isn't it enough for you to
know that if they are not from God, they
will fail after a time?[25]

Do you really know your own motives?
Do you know what it is to protest against
yourselves, as well as others? Do you
examine yourselves to see if you are
patient (for patience means suffering) in
the way demanded by any creative work, by
any act of birth?

I

The violence we find in the peacemaker is creative aggression! It can revolutionise human society, throw out a challenge, make men take a stand. It holds a force which can communicate to all men. There are certain characteristics, too, which belong to it.

First of all, this aggression is a living protest against the blindness of Christian conscience when it tolerates hatred and injustice.

What a challenge is thrown out by the Christian who makes himself a living source of hope in a world of injustice, segregation and starvation! Because he is devoid of hatred, his presence can only be constructive, not destructive; his presence is creativity itself. His challenge to the world is made passionate by love; his is an aggression in which love dwells, and when a man's life is inflamed by a passion of that intensity, he cannot help but start a fire raging on earth.

DIARY

At Taizé, we have tried to use aggression against the conscience of the Christian world which has tolerated separations in faith and allowed itself to be shaped and hardened by divisions.

Our aggression has been prolonged and unceasing; we have searched for the right language, as well, to express our protest.

This protest finds its expression and, in addition, a way of being positively active which can't be compared to anything else, in our community prayer and in our singing of the psalms.

Another characteristic of the violence in the peacemaker is that his aggression is a way of persevering throughout life in intimacy with the life of another, the life of the resurrected Christ. If Christ finds us faithful unto death, He Himself then rewards our perseverance by offering us an intimacy which fills our entire being and gives us true life.

Those who receive this gift can perceive something else beyond the concrete world of events and objects which surrounds us, something beyond our immediate hopes and desires, something deeper and more intimate to us. Here He waits. Here we shall find Him as we take our stand before Him. Here He waits for us.

DIARY

This morning, as we came away from community prayer, a brother whispered in my ear: 'Martin Luther King has been assassinated.'

For us, and particularly for our brothers in Chicago, his death means the loss of a friend. Where will armed aggression lead us to, if it is now killing the best of men among us?

The thought of what will become of the black people now they have lost their prophet haunts me?

He was a messenger to men. He was an advocate of non-violence. The phrase isn't a happy one, but it has been coined and it is as well to use it. Yet all men are violent, all men are aggressive, Martin Luther King included. But he used his aggression in such a disinterested way that the power of Another could be seen in it.

Peacemakers use their aggression to break the chain-reactions set off by abuses of power in our time, power which disguises a kind of aggression which we cannot tolerate, an aggression which subjects the poor and oppresses them. By giving up his life for his friends,[27] Martin Luther King has opened a path into the future. No one will have the strength to close that path in our faces.

But it is a path full of dangers. He knew this himself: 'I have been buffeted by storms of persecution, I have to confess that at times it seemed to me I couldn't go on carrying such a burden any longer. Now I have found that the burden the master places on us is light, above all when we take up his yoke ourselves.'[28]

His death has led me to search for a meaning in my own death. If man cannot find a meaning for his death, he cannot really live.

For some, death is brutal. Others lose their lives by wasting away, from undernourishment, without work to save them. Some, too, whose lives are devoted to caring for a family, die a slow death, suffering in themselves the bitterness which fills those closest to them.

I was talking for almost three hours to a revolutionary student. He would like to

see a society founded on justice, springing from what is good and spontaneous in
men. Utopia, for him, is a valuable
concept; it represents our urge to
create.

But at the same time, he affirmed
harshly that the death of Martin Luther
King was beneficial. It will release
a lot of forces. He thought that King was
obstructing the road to freedom, he was
channelling the explosive forces of
aggression and confining them. Without
him, boiling-point can be reached this
summer in the United States and there can
be real destruction; this will produce an
impact in Europe.

I listen to him speaking, and his words
cause a wound in me which bleeds. And as I
listen, I question myself and ask myself
how much in me is inconsequential, how
much in me a form of unsuspected
sectarianism, when he, talking to me, can
display such signs without being aware of
them.

Prophecy, its Importance Today

A ray of hope illuminates the life of the Church. We can see
signs of this in the great, irreversible changes which are taking
place. Sometimes, though, we are confused by the complexity
of events; we cannot easily see from what is happening today
what tomorrow will bring to Christian life. But life goes on –
life which is vital, in this case. Yes, prophecy still has a vital
importance.

Christians, who have been divided for centuries, cannot afford to ignore one another any longer. The new generation of Christians does not want us to present ourselves before non-believers divided as we are at the moment. Young Christians are examining themselves, even when their dialogue hasn't any immediate fruit.

For these young people, God is not dead. What they *do* refuse to accept, and aggressively, is false dialogue, and the clichés uttered by their elders. When, however, these older folk succeed in expressing themselves in new terms, they are understood as never before by the young. But how can we destroy the notion in some of them that the older generation can be completely rejected? The point of reference sought by young people is our human experience gained in life; here, of course, age is irrelevant. But youngsters are ready to see that, by wanting to build alone, they can create nothing. Without the contribution each one of us makes daily, nothing could survive in human society.

For them, friendship is not an empty word. They understand friendship as an act of sharing. Through their efforts, tomorrow's Church is taking shape; small cells of activity are springing up everywhere in which the spirit of working together and creating in common has a reality never before witnessed.

These cells are made up of young married couples or young unmarried people, girls or boys. Those who are unmarried sacrifice a period of their life to a 'sandwich' vocation, to what amounts to a real call to celibacy, which they pursue for a space of time.

There may be aspects of this spontaneous, but creative, work which challenge and embarrass the Church, but, in almost every case, those who undertake it have a real sense of belonging to the Church.[29]

DIARY

These last few days, the greater part of
the country has been immobilised by
strikes.

The situation saddens us. When it began,
we felt somewhat empty and frustrated at
not being directly involved. But little by
little I began to see the genuine validity
of living one's entire life before God
and searching within oneself for justice.
In the light of the situation, what
suggestion could I make to my brothers
here? That some of them should go off
daily to work in the factories? Some of
us, in other continents, are already
working amongst the poorest levels of
society, as labourers, in many cases. For
the last twelve years one of our
brothers here at Taizé has been working
with the local countryfolk and helping
them to progress. His activities have
been strongly criticised from the
outside. Here, where we try to pursue
the end of reconciliation, have we the
strength to risk stirring up even more
misunderstanding in the minds of others?

Some of these questions I put to the
young married couples with whom I often
discuss our life and possible ways of
changing it. They are astonished to hear
me say that their remarks and comments
can be valuable to our community. They
don't fully realise the impact that the

dialogue between us can have on our life
here. And yet, surely we are all of us
fighting the same struggle? Unfortunately,
we have too little faith in what we can
give others.

We then talked about a preoccupation of
their own. Hasn't the time come, we
thought, for them to set up a new basis
for relationships within their own
community, by forming some kind of union
between their homes? Their life, like ours
is governed by a pattern of habits, and by
sharing together as fully as possible, by
praying together, they can transform this
life completely. We, here, will depend
on them for support; they, in their turn,
will depend on us.

Small lay-brotherhoods of this kind are formed spontaneously; no one wants them to have the rigid character of
institutions. Their days are numbered when they begin; they
are essentially provisional, and this is a characteristic they
recognise and bow to, even if it means disbanding. For this
very reason, small groups like this can be an animating force
within existing church institutions.

Their life is one of commitment in a secular society, but
they acknowledge the source of their inspiration by eating
meals of friendship together, or even, sometimes, by cele-
brating the Eucharist in their homes.

Because they reflect hope and joy, they are a living proof
that Christians are not just a self-pitying bunch of people.

And if these groups can come to depend on a neighbouring
community of men who are also committed for life, the possibilities for both sides become enormous.

As for the religious community itself, it is a meeting-place for the world at large. In its common prayer and Eucharist, it offers an atmosphere of celebration – in a festive sense – which all liturgy contains. At weekends and holidays, when people as a whole tend to satisfy their nomadic instincts, they can gather together at celebrations such as we can offer here; here, in groups or individually, they can experience the joys of sharing and the joys of real communion between men.

In the same way, in the cities, there will always be vast churches where people will congregate in large numbers. This is most evident in the winter-season.

These, and other, experiences we have of society help us to form a picture in our minds of the Church of tomorrow.

DIARY

When I saw our new concrete church going up, there was something about it which bothered me. Even now, years later, I still haven't come to accept it very readily. I would rather the building were half-buried in the earth, and less visible to the eyes of men.

True, we have set about constructing our community here with a view to permanency, but our modern society has such mobility that perhaps we should look on the Church's life as though it were permanently 'under canvas'.

Last winter we removed all the harsher and harder lines in the interior of the church, and – concrete or no concrete – we managed to arrive at a more fluid and more

elastic design inside the church. But the
exterior remains unchanged. What can we
do? Surround it with trees?

All the same, we have learnt a lot from
the experience. Concrete makes a building
rigid and forceful.

Isn't the first duty of Christians in our time to create brotherhood?

In the early Church, this was the guiding force: Christians
persevered together, welcomed one another, ate together.
They were filled, irresistibly, with a spirit of celebration. In
their work, in their hardship, they shared everything. There
was no pressure on anyone to adapt himself to a common
mould; they were all as one, but there was pluralism in their
oneness.[30]

More than that, they were not a community like any other,
but a gathering of men amongst whom the resurrected Christ
was present.

DIARY

I was answering questions from a group of
some forty girls. A young girl asks me,
in a fresh and timid voice I can hardly
hear: 'How, with our little knowledge,
can we hope to penetrate a world as
complex as it is today?'

I answered: Every man, every woman,
no matter how broad or deep his
knowledge, is given a living word,
sometimes no more than one word. By turning this word into action we equip
ourselves to hold within us everything

that is going on in the world around us.

This word we possess makes us close to men everywhere; it opens our minds to the people of China, Cuba, the Eastern countries, the United States, so that we can all work to create the opportunity for all men who are separated to come together.

Back in my room, I continue the train of thought in my own mind.

Man is born for hope. For man, everything in life can be made new.[31]

At a given time in our life, in the midst of our darkness, a living word will bring light. This word opens our being to other men, and we cannot resist.[32]

Christ, though, does not force us to give Him our loyalty.

The Gospel is not a way of enclosing our conscience and the conscience of others in the same framework, within the pattern of a system. It is a way of communion.

By appearing to us in the person of Christ, God accepted poverty and obscurity. The sign of God's presence is not human grandeur, and God does not demand great deeds which are beyond us. He asks simply that we should understand how to love our fellow-humans.

In recent years we have seen the signs of a new birth: the Church of tomorrow is advancing towards unity.

Prophecy still has a tremendous importance, and in the midst of the violence surrounding us today, there is hope which is alive and challenging.

NOTES

A THIRD ALTERNATIVE

1. Apocalypse 3:16.
2. Matthew 11:12.

IT'S OUT OF DATE!

1. Rule of Taizé, p. 74, inspired by Mark 10:29.
2. Paul VI speaking at the Franciscan General Chapter, 23 June 1967: in *Evangile Aujourd'hui* No. 57, p. 56.
3. Ephesians 4:9.
4. 1 Peter 3:19–20.
5. Ephesians 3:18.
6. Matthew 11:12.
7. Luke 17:10.
8. 1 Corinthians 3:9
9. Psalm 126:5.
10. Mark 9:24.
11. These were the terms used by Mgr Marty during a television broadcast at the time of his nomination as Archbishop of Paris.
12. Hebrews 4:12.
13. Matthew 5:9.
14. Madame Marc Boegner.
15. 1 Corinthians 7:20.
16. Apocalypse 2:10.
17. See Isaiah 55:10–11.
18. Marc Oraison, 'Le débat sur le célibat des prêtres', in *Le Monde*, 10 April 1968.

THE WAY OUT

1. Saint Ambrose, 'Treatise on the Gospel of St Luke'.

2. Jonathan Swift, 'Thoughts on Various Subjects'.

3. Speech given by Paul VI to close the Council, 7 December 1965.

4. John XXIII, in a speech addressed to parish priests of Rome on 29 January 1959.

5. Ezekiel 36:26.

6. 'Schema of Documents prepared for each section of the Fourth Assembly of the World Council of Churches', Uppsala, 1968. The whole passage is as follows: 'The Church is Catholic because the Holy Spirit is present and active throughout Her. At the same time, the Church is called on to renew her Catholic nature continually . . . The Holy Spirit urges the Church to contest the frontiers which separate men and, thus, to be a leaven in society, giving witness to the will of God that mankind should be renewed and united . . . But men abuse their freedom and refuse the gift of catholicity individually as well as collectively. This refusal can be seen whenever Christians allow the unity and catholicity of the Church to be replaced by other loyalties and by divisions the world has set up. Examples of this refusal and examples of the deformity it causes are known to all of us. The clearest deformity can be seen where obedience to the Gospels has been overshadowed by confessional and ecclesiastical loyalties which keep Christians in disunity.'

7. See the prayer after communion in the Mass for unity: 'This communion within your mysteries, Lord, prefigures the unity of the faithful within You. Grant that it may create unity in your Church.'

8. Matthew 18:20.

9. Matthew 26:26–29.

10. The clearest statement of this repentance came from Pope Paul when he said: 'If, amongst the causes of our separation, there is fault which can be imputed to us, we humbly ask God's pardon and also the pardon of our brothers whom we may have offended.' Speech given at the opening of the second session of the Council (29 September 1963); in Documentation Catholique No. 1410, col. 1356.

11. See Matthew 13:24–30.

ON THE OTHER SIDE: HOPE

1. Colossians 1:27.
2. 2 Thessalonians 1:3.
3. *Idem*.
4. Matthew 17:20.
5. John 20:29.
6. Colossians 1:27.
7. Matthew 11:12.
8. Matthew 8:8.
9. Ephesians 6:12.
10. Ephesians 6:13.
11. Luke 11:34.
12. Prayer before communion in the Latin liturgy: 'Lord Jesus Christ, who said to your apostles, My peace I leave with you, my peace I give to you, look not upon my sins but on the faith of your Church and grant to her the peace and unity you have always desired.'
13. 'Schema of Documents prepared for each section of the Fourth Assembly of the World Council of Churches', Uppsala, 1968.
14. Saint John Chrysostom.
15. There are 40,000 computers in the United States, 3,000 in the U.S.S.R.
16. Matthew 7:21.
17. Pastoral Constitution on the Church in the Modern World, 'Gaudium et Spes', conclusion, Chapter 93.
18. Colossians 1:24.
19. Martin Luther King, *Chaos or Community?* Hodder and Stoughton, 1968. pp. 102–3.
20. Matthew 5:9.
21. See Luke 9:62.
22. Matthew 26:52.
23. Paul VI, Encyclical, 'Populorum Progression', Part One, Chapter 2, paragraph 31.

The whole of paragraphs 30 and 31 is as follows:

'There are certainly instances when injustice cries out to heaven for repayment. When an entire population, deprived of very essentials, live in such dependence that all initiative and responsibility is forbidden them, as well as all possibility of cultural progress and participation in social and political life, great is the temptation to rise up with violence against such offences against human dignity.

'We are aware, nevertheless that revolutionary aggression – except when men are subjected to clear and prolonged tyranny which could constitute a grave threat to basic human rights and seriously harm the common good of a country – can give rise to new injustices, provoke fresh disorders and cause further ruin. One must not fight a genuine evil at the price of incurring worse disasters.'

See, too, the following passage in the 'Schema of Documents prepared for each section of the Fourth Assembly of the World Council of Churches', Uppsala, 1968: 'Certain convinced Christians believe that it is their duty to resist by having recourse, if necessary, to violence. They risk their lives in a revolutionary attack against established injustice. Others believe that the only authentic Christian witness is borne by non-violence, and they are ready to suffer for their convictions. We believe that both of these attitudes can manifest the agape.'

24. Luke 23:39–43.

25. Acts 5:38.

26. Apocalypse 2:10.

27. See John 15:13.

28. Martin Luther King, quoted in *Le Monde*, 6 April 1968.

29. When we had an international gathering of 1600 young people here at Taizé, one or two older men showed that they understood how patiently the young are waiting. The Cardinal of Bourges, President of the French Bishops, emphasised the prophetic character of the small ecumenical cells we see today. As for Dr. Carson Blake, secretary general of the World Council of Churches, he said to them: 'What is wrong with the Church is that she sometimes proclaims the Gospel in words when she should be proclaiming it in actions.'

30. See Acts 2:42–7 and Acts 4:32–5.

31. See 2 Corinthians 5:17 and Apocalypse 21:5.

32. See Psalm 119:130.